To: David & Marjorie.

My good friends

Jean Faulkner

A WIFE ON THE OCEAN WAVES

GW00455622

Jean Faulkner wrote this book in her mid-twenties when she was travelling with her husband on board Merchant Navy shipping manned by Officers of Sir William Reardon Smith line of Cardiff, South Wales.

After 7 years on the sea, Jean became a mother in 1984. She then worked 10 years as a school dinner lady and 3 years as a Doctor's Receptionist. Unfortunately she became ill in 2000 and has struggled with M.E. over many years. She now lives with her husband in Reading, Berkshire. She is a Christian and Jean believes that the following Psalm is a good description of her time at sea:

PSALM 170 V 23 to 29

They that go down to the sea in ships, that do business in great waters,
These see the works of the Lord, and his wonders in the deep
For He commandeth and raiseth the stormy wind, which lifteth up the waves thereof.
They mount up to the heavens, they go down again to the depths, their soul is melted because of trouble.
They reel to and fro, and stagger like a drunken man, and are at their wit's end
Then they cry unto the Lord in their troubles, and He bringeth them out of their distresses.
He maketh the storm a calm, so that the waves thereof are still.

A WIFE ON THE OCEAN WAVES

Jean Faulkner

A WIFE ON THE OCEAN WAVES

Olympia Publishers
London

www.olympiapublishers.com
OLYMPIA PAPERBACK EDITION

A CIP catalogue record for this title is
available from the British Library.

ISBN: 978-1-84897-156-1

First Published in 2011

Olympia Publishers
60 Cannon Street
London
EC4N 6NP

Printed in Great Britain

Contents

INTRODUCTION

Fate is a very powerful thing. Even in my wildest dreams, I did not foresee that by the time I was twenty-four I would have visited numerous foreign countries and spent eleven months on board ships at sea. But, fate arranged it for me, and very simply too.

In 1971, I met Colin. At the time, he was an electrical apprentice but less than a year later, he joined the Merchant Navy as a deck cadet and sailed off for six months on his first voyage to sea. Over the next two years, we established a long-distance relationship and as soon as Colin passed his exams to become a Second Mate, we were married.

Fate had already arranged about ten years previously that wives could accompany Merchant Navy Officers on their trips to sea, so there I was, a farmer's daughter, whose total experience of travel was a few weeks on school trips, visiting countries as diverse as Argentina and Taiwan. I thanked fate for giving me this opportunity.

On the first trip to sea, I visited Denmark; Argentina; Taiwan; Korea; the United States of America; Panama and Germany. I was too busy adjusting to this strange way of life and enjoying numerous exciting experiences to think of writing a book but I did write long and detailed accounts of my exploits in letters to friends and family. Later, I learnt that these letters were received and read with great enthusiasm and interest, so, I began to wonder whether I should write about my experiences more permanently in the form of a book. So on my second trip to sea I wrote this book.

I found that writing a book was far more difficult than writing letters home. At the time, I could not decide whether I was making a fair interpretation of the things that I saw and did. However, one day I read the following passage by a very experienced true-life authoress, Pearl S Buck, and it made me feel much better about what I was doing. She wrote in her book' China as I see it' 'The only rule for an interpreter, if one feels he must be an interpreter of something, is to tell faithfully, what he has seen and what he thinks he knows, continually remembering and saying that he is only one person and that he is liable to error.'

Finally, I must thank all the officers and crew on M.V. Amparo during those dates and the Shipping Company for, unknowingly, being subjects of my book. I do not mention many names for, I do not think it necessary, but I thank them all and hope that everyone who reads my book finds some entertainment and even a little knowledge.

CHAPTER 1

JOURNEY TO MEXICO

I awoke at 4.30 a.m. on 18th October 1977. I hadn't really slept deeply all night and suddenly I was wide awake.

I knew that, within a couple of hours, Colin (my husband) and I would be leaving the relative security of our recently acquired home on the first stage of a journey to Guaymas Mexico. There we were to join the M.V. Amparo, our new home for five months. I couldn't help feeling excited at the prospect, but I was also a bit apprehensive. During the previous weeks I had cleared the house of valuables, packed away dust collectors and cleaned everything left and now, after turning off the electricity, gas and water we were ready to leave. My brother, who had kindly offered to drive us to Heathrow airport to save us carrying our luggage on trains and buses, picked us up a little after 6.00 a.m. and we left on the first stage of our long journey.

It was very foggy, and chilly, in fact a typical early autumn morning in England, and it was nice to think that in a matter of hours we would be basking in the sun. As dawn arrived the fog lifted a little but the journey was inevitably slow and we were glad we had left ourselves plenty of time. We were to meet the rest of the ship's new officers at one of the big hotels near Heathrow, where they had stayed overnight. Nearly three quarters of an hour later we were entering the Sheraton Hotel, Heathrow. The lobby was large and imposing and filled with uniformed porters; residents reading early morning newspapers and casually strewn suitcases. I had never met any of our future colleagues before but I could identify them at once. It was difficult to know why they were so conspicuous but obviously, being so many men on their own had something to do with it. They seemed to have an air of resignation about them as well as a suppressed excitement about the following five months. Most of them looked as if they had enjoyed a few drinks the night before as they, inevitably swapped tales of previous voyages and tried to forget that they were leaving behind their homes and families.

We introduced ourselves and, after bidding farewell to my brother, we sat back to wait for the fog to clear. It didn't take long and by 9.30 a.m. we were boarding a coach that was to take us to the airport.

I had spent many hours at Heathrow over the previous years, waiting for Colin to return from one trip or other, so I was familiar with the airport buildings. They hadn't changed and were still full of cosmopolitan atmosphere and hundreds of people walking; scurrying; sitting and enquiring. An agent for the Shipping Company made the travel arrangements for us and as soon as we had checked in, handed over our hoards of papers and been searched, our flight was boarding and the second stage of our journey was about to begin.

The plane was a 747 Jumbo Jet, a massive craft which, I was told, could carry three hundred passengers. I had never been aboard one before and I was amazed by its size. I couldn't help wondering how on earth it got off the ground. It did, however, with relative ease and soon we were soaring over England and away to the west and America. The flight took seven hours. We were given a meal of chicken, vegetables, salad, ice-cream and coffee and entertained by a rather mediocre film. I was surprised how quickly the time went and we soon found ourselves descending and the pilot informed us of the five hour time difference and our imminent arrival. Before landing we banked over New York and then we were rushing headlong past the marsh land that surrounds the runways at John F. Kennedy Airport.

We had a four hour wait at New York before our next flight to Mexico City. That time did not go very quickly. We wandered about, changed some money, and had a drink and eventually went to the Departure Lounge ready to board flight 401. At 5.45 p.m., New York time, we left terra firma again and soared into the air. It was soon dark and, after a delicious meal accompanied by free champagne, I settled back to doze. The next thing I knew was we were flying over the huge twinkling night-time panorama of Mexico City.

After landing we made our way to another Arrivals Lounge. By the time we arrived at the Custom's desk we had been travelling over twenty hours. We all felt extremely weary and when we learnt that we were to take a few hours sleep at a nearby hotel there were sighs of relief all round. The relief, however, was short-lived when we found that we were to be held up at the Custom's desk,

Each of our party had a special letter from the Shipping Company explaining the purpose of visiting the country to ensure easy movement through Customs but these did not satisfy the officials. It was very frustrating but quite a common occurrence according to one of our

Companions who said he'd been to Mexico several times and each time the officials wanted different papers. Eventually, after at least half an hour's heated discussion, it was decided that an entry visa had to be completed by each individual. This took a further half an hour but finally we were allowed through. We were led, sleepily to waiting minibuses for a hair-raising dash through the city. The minibus drivers were obviously racing one another as they dashed into any lane in order to be the first to the destination. Through the fog of sleep, it seemed that everyone else was driving just as, madly, but I thought I must be dreaming when I saw that a police car had a rubber bumper like a dodgem car at the fair, all around itself! In the morning I saw that it was true and quite necessary.

By some miracle we reached the hotel safely, although it was only an average sort of place it seemed like paradise itself. After twenty-two hours travelling it was wonderful to have a bed to collapse onto. I slept like a log until about 6.00 a.m. when first light drifted across the mountains and the sounds of the immense city (including whistles; screeching brakes and horns) started the symphony of the day! We had breakfast at 7.00 a.m; no one knew what the rest of the day had in store for us. We were soon to find that out. Straight after breakfast, the same minibus drivers collected us from the hotel and tore at breakneck speed back across the City. At each road junction a smartly dressed policeman stood with a whistle in his hand and he risked life and limb by leaping out in front of the traffic blowing his whistle and waving every time he wanted to let cars in from side roads. While we were stopped I was able to get a fleeting glance of Mexico City. There were many unfamiliar sights but two things seemed especially strange. The first were the shoe shine boys. I had never seen one before but here were hundreds of them, each sitting on the pavement below their chairs busily shining their client's shoes. The other strange sight was the shops. They were all closed off from the street by huge metal pull-down doors and looked more like garages than shops. The speed of our drivers ensured that our journey didn't take long and all too soon we were back in the departure lounge at the airport. I don't know whether it was the hair-raising drive or jet lag but as we waited in the lounge a horrible feeling of nausea overcame me and when the flight was called it took all my efforts to make it to the plane. I did, however and by the time we were airborne and strange sights were passing underneath, interest took over and I felt much better. I hoped that the plane would take us all the way to Guaymas but we soon learned that our destination was Hermisillo. During the flight the plane stayed at a fairly low altitude and there was very little cloud so I was able to get a good look at the Mexican terrain. Mexico City itself had looked enormous at night but now, in daylight, it looked even bigger. The blocks of houses stretched from one horizon to the other and it was a long time before we left them all behind. Then we passed over mountains which looked, from such a height, like grey sand piles which were divided by irregular lines drawn by invisible fingers. These lines, the valleys, had many, what I thought were tracks running down them. I realised, however, that these tracks were dry river beds.

After half an hour's flying the scenery below changed into flat desert and we were soon landing at Hermisillo. It could barely be described as an airport as it only had one short runway and a shed for a terminal. The pilot had to turn the plane round and taxi back to the shed. There were no covered entrances to the building and as we stepped out of the plane onto the tarmac we immediately realised a vast difference in the temperature. It had been quite chilly in Mexico City because of its altitude and I was quite surprised it was so hot. It felt as if someone had thrown a warm blanket around my shoulders; it was a very nice feeling.

The arrival of a plane must have been one of the big events of the day as the terminal building was crowded with chattering excited people. They were not waiting for anyone specific but were just interested in us all, while we waited for our luggage to arrive from the plane, eyes peered at us from all directions and numerous enthusiastic tanned men asked if we wanted our photos taken. It was a bit disconcerting and I was quite glad when our luggage arrived and an agent from the Shipping Company led us outside. Once we were outside he asked us to wait for a moment and disappeared behind the building. After a while he returned on the oldest bus I have ever seen in my life! Its square body was composed of twenty per cent rust and eighty per cent dents and we all stared in disbelief as the agent waved us aboard. There was no luggage compartment at the back so we formed a line along the bus and each piece of luggage was passed along the line. Now that we were inside we could see that the metal seats had no padding and when we sat down on them we realised that we had a very uncomfortable ride ahead of us. I am sure that if we had known that Guaymas was over seventy miles away across the desert, some of us would have turned round and got off again! The temperature, now that it was approaching midday was over 90 degrees Fahrenheit and yet even to imagine that such a bus had air conditioning would be absurd. All we could do was open the few windows that weren't jammed solid and sit back and sweat out the journey. The town of Hermisillo was only small and consisted of gatherings of square single-storied houses surrounded by wasteland and rubbish. It wasn't long therefore, before we left it behind and the scene changed to barren desert. In fact, the view from the dusty bus windows looked just like a set from some old cowboy movie. On each horizon a gaunt mountain of red rock stood as a jagged landmark and from mountain to mountain stretched acre upon acre of sand. Here and there, a cactus, a stunted tree or an outcrop of coarse grass stuck out from the sand in defiance of the climate, and circling above the cactus lone eagles soared, scanning the sand for rodents. Thankfully the road was a relatively modern tarmac-ed highway but even so the bus shuddered and groaned and at top speed, forty miles an hour, the driver had difficulty holding the steering wheel steady. He had brought his entire family with him, his wife; small daughter and older son, and, when he got tired of driving he let his son take over for a while. Every now and then we passed a wooden shack at the roadside. These shacks were the homes of ranchers who, somehow, gleaned a living from small herds of sturdy cattle that managed to find enough to eat in the surrounding desert. The grander of the ranch shacks were built of wood and had corrals alongside them. But some were merely heaps of corrugated iron and scrap thrown together to give shelter against the elements.

When we had been travelling for over an hour I finally realised that our journey was going to be a long one as we stopped at one of the roadside shacks which advertised refreshments. The driver and all the family got out of the bus and disappeared inside the shack without a word. When they returned, about ten minutes later, the driver filled the radiator from a bottle of water and drove on again still without uttering a word!

We drove on and on across the desert, eventually reaching a once-distant mountain only to see another one just as far away.

Eventually, when we began to wonder if we would ever get there we arrived at Guaymas, the docks and the M.V. Amparo.

CHAPTER 2

THE M.V. AMPARO AND SHIPBOARD LIFE

The M.V. (motor vessel) Amparo was a general cargo vessel. She was only 11,410.45 tons gross weight and, therefore, small by comparison with modern super tankers and bulk carriers, but she looked large enough to me as she lay alongside the quay. She was owned by a Mexican firm: Transportation Maritima Mexicana S.A. (T.M.M. for short), although on mortgage from a Panamanian firm. When we arrived T.M.M.'s red and green house flag was flying from the monkey island mast. She had been built in Bremerhaven, Germany in 1967 but from the quayside showed few outward signs of her ten years hard work.

As we climbed wearily up the gangway, stretching our aching travel-sore muscles we could see she had six holds, four serviced by derricks and two by cranes. The conglomerate of ropes and posts, around the lifting gear, above her decks, made her look like an olden day's sailing ship, minus sails! Once on deck we had a quick glance around and then made our way towards the after end accommodation.

The present ship's officers were all British and employed by the same company as Colin, to manage the M.V. Amparo for the Mexicans. They were eagerly awaiting our arrival, knowing that, as soon as the formalities of handing over were completed, they would be off on the first stage of their homeward journey. They had already been away for over five months and their excitement was obvious.

As Colin was to sail as Third Mate we were shown the Third Mate's cabin which was small and crowded with a bunk; wardrobe; table; desk; and daybed so when we were informed that the much larger cabin next door was free and we could use that, I was very relieved.

Eventually the handover was completed and the paying off officers rushed down the gangway laden with souvenirs; cases; and bottles of spirits; to the waiting taxis, our bus having miraculously disappeared as easily as it had appeared!

At last I was able to collapse and view our surroundings. The new cabin was very comfortable. It had a separate day room, as well as a bedroom and a bathroom. The outside corridor opened into the dayroom, which contained a large writing desk; a table; two chairs; a daybed; a wardrobe and a fridge. The dayroom led through into the bedroom, which was very small but adequate containing a double bunk and a wardrobe.

The bathroom, which was next to the bedroom was also small but functional, and had a shower as well as a washbasin and toilet.

The cabin was on the starboard corner of the ship's superstructure and the portholes looked forward and to the side. I was especially pleased to have forward-looking portholes as I remembered that I had felt claustrophobic on the previous ship when we had had a cabin with a solitary side-facing porthole.

Now that I was back on the ship again I started to remember the shipboard jargon, which I had previously learnt, and how important it was. I knew, to my cost, that if one used shore-side words for shipboard things one was liable to forfeit a case of beer to the other officers. I racked my brain to remember all the proper words.

I remembered that a wall was a bulkhead; the floor was the deck; the ceiling was the deck head; the corridors were alleyways and beds had to be called bunks. The settees or couches were daybeds and the windows portholes. There were numerous other expressions and words used throughout the ship. The kitchens were the galleys; the dining room was called the saloon; and the lounge, the smoke room! Of course one had to call left port and right starboard. Being upstairs was being topside; downstairs was below and outside was on deck. The strangest expression of all was the one used for a trip ashore, this was: going up the road.

Whilst I was unpacking I suddenly remembered that the Ship's personnel had 'jargon' names too. The Captain was known as The Old Man; the radio officer was the Sparky; the Chief Engineer was the Chief whereas the Chief Deck Officer was the Mate. The second, third and fourth etc engineers were known as the 2nd, 3rd, and 4th whereas the second third and fourth mates had their full title 2nd Mate; 3rd. Mate and 4th Mate. The Chief Steward was the Grocer and finally the electrician was the Lecky.

It wasn't long before everything was unpacked and put away and soon it was time for the evening meal-dinner. I was very hungry, as I hadn't eaten anything since a piece of toast at breakfast.

The saloon was on the deck above our cabin and when Colin and I arrived there, soon after being summoned by a nifty tune on a xylophone, most of the other officers were there too. The saloon was very well laid out and contained two long tables and a sideboard where the stewards kept the cutlery; sauces etc. The lower half of the deck heads were wooden panelling, and, hanging on one of them, was a picture of a member of the

Swedish Royal Family (we never did find out exactly who!) placed there by the previous owners of the ship, a Swedish firm.

I think that the quality of the food and service in ship always amazes the layman and I know that, on my first visit to a ship, I had expected the meals to be served up 'canteen' style and was most surprised to find silver service waiters and a choice of food from several courses. The M.V. Amparo was no exception and that evening we sat at a beautifully laid out table and ate a choice of food from five different courses, which included T-bone steak! After the meal there was a short social meeting in the bar and then everyone disappeared for an early night which I, for one, really appreciated.

We stayed at Guaymas for another three days and during that time I familiarised myself with the ship and its occupants. On board the Amparo there were fourteen British officers; thirty-one Indian crew; as well as another wife and myself. All the officers were new to the ship except the Chief Steward (and his wife) who had already been on the ship for a month. The crew had been on board since April. I knew that both officers and crew, on board ship, were divided roughly into two departments. One department was in charge of navigation and cargo and was called the Deck Department. The other was in charge of the engines and was called the Engineering Department! The Captain; Mate; the Second Mate and the Third Mate (Colin) were the Deck Officers. The Engineering Officers were the Chief; the 2nd; the 3rd, two 4ths; and a junior 4th. There was also an engineering cadet for a few weeks before he transferred to another ship. There was also a Radio Officer; and Electrician and a Chief Steward who didn't really fit into either department.

The crew were also divided into departments but as well as Deck and Engineering Department there was also a Catering one. On deck there was a Deck Serang (in charge); a Deck Cassab/Tindal (second in charge); three Seamen/Helmsmen, known as Secunys; eight general Seamen and a Deck Utility Hand. The engine room had an Engine Room Serang (in charge) and Engine Room Tindal/Cassab (second in charge) five donkeymen/greasers and a Chippy (carpenter) The Catering Department was made up of a Cook/Baker and a Second Cook, who did the Officers' cooking; a Pantryman, who helped the cooks; three General Stewards, who served the meals and cleaned the accommodation; a Bhandary and a Bhandary's Mate, who cooked for the crew; a Laundryman and another Utility Hand.

I familiarised myself with the accommodation simply by walking about in it! The M.V. Amparo had five accommodation decks situated at her after end and above the engine room around the funnel. The lowest deck was the

Lower Poop Deck and above that, on the same level as the outside main deck was the Poop Deck. These two decks housed the crew's accommodation; the laundry rooms; the galley; the crew's mess room and their activities room. I knew that I would not see much of these two decks because, as crew's decks they were kept separate from the officer's accommodation. I knew also that I would probably only get to know the three stewards from the crew and although others I would know by sight some I would not meet at all.

Our cabin was situated on the next deck up called the promenade deck. Most of the officers' accommodation was on this deck as well as the library room; the bar and the hospital. The hospital was a small cabin next to ours and it contained a cupboard full of pills and bottles and a number of bunk beds. The bar was also a small cabin but, as such, was very cosy and plenty large enough to accommodate all of the officers. There was a small wooden-topped bar in one corner which had a refrigerator; a sink unit; and a glass/bottle rack behind it. Above the bar was an ingenious row of coloured lights which had been placed for decoration. There were several stools fixed to the floor around the bar as well as a number of easy chairs and daybeds. For entertainment there was a dartboard. The bar looked out forward through four large portholes. I learnt later that some of the engineers, who had just joined, had built the bar after the original bar had been removed when the Mexicans bought the ship. They claimed that the bar was in fact the Captain's bathroom door!

The next deck up was called the Boat Deck because the lifeboats were situated there. This deck housed the Chief's and the Mate's cabins and also the Smoke Room; Salon; and Pantry. The Pantry was just a small room which contained a service lift to the galley and a refrigerator. This room was the Pantryman's domain and it was his job to co-ordinate the food with the orders. At night, the Pantry was left open and we were able to make sandwiches and snacks from the food left in the refrigerator. The Smoke Room was alongside the Saloon and could be entered through sliding doors between the two rooms or by a doorway from the alleyway. The Smoke Room was designed for use as a games room and reading room but was only used, while I was on the Amparo, for watching video films or television, while in port. The real social centre of the ship was the bar.

The Bridge Deck above the boat deck housed the Captain's cabin, the Radio Officer's cabin and the Supercargo, Pilot and Owner's suite. The latter three were used very occasionally and only once whilst I was on board, when the Owner's Suite was used by a Mexican passenger.

The topmost deck, excluding the Monkey Island, (which was simply a bulkhead used for sunbathing and radar equipment) was the Bridge Deck.

This was the nerve centre of navigation. On the Amparo the bridge contained the wheel; magnetic and gyro compasses; communication equipment; fire alarm equipment; the telegraph (which, indicated to the Engine Room the speed required for instance: dead slow; full ahead etc.) two radar sets; lights consul; VHF radio set; aldis lamp; and an echo sounder be sides many displayed lists explaining such details as operation of equipment and locality of fire hydrants. The whole forward bulkhead of the bridge had portholes in it giving as wide a range of vision as possible and there were also bridge wings on either side, which, being extensions to the deck, gave extra sideways as well as reverse vision. The bridge could be closed off from the bridge wings by shutting two sliding doors. Behind and on one side of the bridge was the chart room, which housed all the chart; reference books; date and numerical tables, which were needed for safe navigation as well as a large table to hold the charts. Behind the bridge on the other side was the Radio Room, which was full of electrical equipment, radio receivers and a weather facsimile machine. I knew that shipboard life, in port was totally different from that at sea. In fact, there was no real routine at all but while we were alongside it gave everyone an opportunity to get accustomed to the ship. Having been to sea before I knew that while in port the Engineers generally did 'day work' from 8.30 a.m. to 5.00 p.m. repairing and maintaining the engines while they were not in use. The Deck department's working hours in port were very flexible. It was Colin's and the Second Mate's duty to do the cargo watches between them and, as such, their working hours depended solely on the working hours of the shore-side stevedores. These could range from twenty-four hours each day down to as little as four hours, and sometimes, very occasionally down to none at all! The Mate was in charge of the loading and unloading and the maintenance of the deck gear and normally did day work while in port. The Captain was in charge of all the paperwork and dealing with the Agents; officials; and representatives, besides having overall responsibility for every activity on the ship. His working hours had to be very flexible. The Radio Officer, like the Engineers, took the opportunity, in port, of maintaining and repairing his equipment. The Chief Steward's hours were also very flexible because besides his normal duties he had to deal with customs; immigration; and stores ordering and delivery.

To me, in port, meant going up the road and I took every opportunity to see the places, which we visited. While in Guaymas that first time, however, I didn't go ashore but, after unpacking and getting acclimatised, I soaked up the beautiful sunshine and watched the fishermen and the pelicans and wondered what the next five months had in store for me, whilst aboard the M.V. Amparo.

CHAPTER 3

MANZANILLO, AND MY FIRST TRIP UP THE ROAD

We left Guaymas for Manzanillo on Saturday 22nd October at 9.30 p.m. It seemed strange to be on the move, but the noise from the engines was minimal, compared with the previous ship I had sailed on and, that night, I slept very soundly.

The first thing I saw when I lifted the blinds in the morning was a group of dolphins playing in the foaming water at the side of the ship. Their black bodies glistened as they leapt in the air and gracefully re-entered the water three yards further on. I had seen dolphins many times before, both in captivity and in the wild, and I knew that they were very intelligent creatures, but it always amazed me to see them using ships as 'playthings!'. They would come from miles around simply to have the 'pleasure' of playing in the bow wave or wake of the ship. I watched them for a long time but, eventually, they tired of that particular game and made off towards the horizon.

The weather was fine although it was quite cloudy and during the morning we saw two waterspouts rising from the sea carrying water up into a black cloud. It looked as if there was a huge vacuum cleaner hidden amongst the billowy cloud, sucking up the sea in a spiral, with tremendous power. Colin told me that water spouts are a sign of unstable weather conditions but the sun shone all day and during the afternoon I improved my suntan. In the evening the clocks were put forward an hour to bring us in line with local time at Manzanillo. There was always a lot of clock changing and although I understood the reason for them I always found it difficult to readjust after losing or gaining an hour. When we gained an hour, each watch (four hours) was extended by twenty minutes so that each watchkeeper did the same amount of extra work. The first twenty minutes went on the Mate's watch, the second on Colin's and the third went on at midnight completing the hour. Of course, the reverse took place when we lost an hour. Colin only changed his watch by forty minutes, to prevent three adjustments, I changed mine the full hour after dinner. Our watches, therefore, showed different times and I was always totally confused until the next day!

There were two clocks in the Chart Room. One showed local times, the other Greenwich Mean Time, because all nautical calculations were worked out using G.M.T. Therefore, I always knew what time it was back in England and, often, I would think of everyone at home going to bed while we were halfway through the morning or getting ready for dinner.

It only took forty hours to reach Manzanillo and we were soon tying up alongside the quay. Our berth was next to a large lagoon and the sandspit that divided the lagoon from the bay was crowded with modern hotels. The actual town of Manzanillo was about a mile away, between high hills and the sea, on the opposite side of the bay. The hills surrounding the bay were sparsely vegetated with trees and coarse grass and, scattered on their slopes, were groups of corrugated iron and wood shacks.

Cargo work was not starting until the following morning so Colin was able to come up the road with me. During the afternoon it was very hot and humid and the thermometer wavered between 90 degrees Fahrenheit and 95 degrees Fahrenheit. We decided to wait until the cool of the evening before walking into town. It was 6.30 p.m. by the time we left the ship and it was just starting to get dark, but the temperature was still 85 degrees Fahrenheit. From the dock gate to the town there were houses strung out in untidy rows. Most of them, unlike the ones on the hillside, were made of concrete and some were far grander than others. In most cases the gardens were used for rubbish dumps as nothing grew unless it was regularly watered.

We passed a doctor's surgery and, by contrast, its garden was very well looked after. It was laid down to lawn with a coconut palm and bushes scattered here and there for effect. Some of the shrubs had vivid coloured flowers on them. I recognised that they were bougainvillea. 'Growing' out of the lawn at regular intervals were taps! They were obviously placed like that to facilitate easy irrigation but they did look strange.

The rickety concrete slab path that led to the town followed the railway lines and with great noise and clamour, huge trains, pulling only a couple of goods carriages, came up from behind us and rattled towards the town. The engines themselves were as large and majestic as our old steam trains but squarer in design. Their cabs were crammed with children taking a free ride, and a few brave teenagers danced along the top of the carriages, as the driver blew the deep sounding air horn to warn passersby of his presence.

Along the side of the rickety path, trees had been planted at regular intervals. Each had a moat dug round it so that it could be watered without the precious water running away into the thin sandy soil surrounding the roots. The leaves of the trees were very large and oily surfaced like the leaves of a rubber plant. Some of the older trees had strange looking fruit growing on them. Some of the fruits I recognised as limes and others looked like giant runner beans.

On the outskirts of the town there were shacks like the ones I'd seen on the hillside. They could only really be described as hovels. They had earth floors and their walls were simply pieces of wood and metal thrown together. Their roofs were made of coconut fronds. Their doors, gaps in the walls, were surrounded by rubbish and, here and there, mangy-looking dogs sniffed around.

In Mexico, as in every other underdeveloped country, poverty showed itself quite clearly. I was appalled at first by the way people lived. I realised that they had never known any other way of life and they certainly did not look unhappy or downtrodden but they were certainly missing out on a lot. Some time later I was talking to a Mexican man about the country and he told me that the Mexican government received a lot of foreign aid to help improve her economy and create work for poor people, so that they could earn a decent wage and raise their standard of living. He explained, however,\that Mexican life was very corrupt and that their livelihood was built around what they could glean from other people. As the aid was given to the top officials they took the largest cut but all the way along the line of authority, down to the poor people, the aid was gradually siphoned off. By the time it arrived at its rightful place, to pay for schools, job creation schemes; health clinics etc., only a small, inadequate amount remained. He said that, apparently, deceit could seldom be proved as the money was always cleverly accounted for, on paper.

Of course, I had no proof of what he said but he seemed to have had first-hand experience of the situation. I wondered if the countries supplying the aid realised the extent of the cheating, but I felt sure that they did. However, there just didn't seem any solution as a whole way of life could not be changed especially when it profited the officials allocating it.

As we passed through the outskirts of Manzanillo we were joined by groups of schoolchildren. It was about 6.30 p.m. by this time, and it appeared that, because of the heat of the afternoon, the schools closed for a siesta and then re-opened again in late afternoon. Now the children were on their way home.

We drifted along surrounded by children, some with their mothers, others holding hands with brothers or sisters or friends. It wasn't long before the crowds thickened and the pavement became jammed with animated people, and we found ourselves in the middle of some festivities. About twelve people dressed in brightly coloured costumes, were dancing to the beat of a drum. They moved up and down the street a number of times and some of the onlookers joined in. They made their way to a local hall which had religious paintings on the walls. Everyone crowded in after them and we were left to continue our walk along virtually deserted pavements.

By this time we were rather lost so I tried out my Spanish, which I had only just begun to learn. Needless to say I wasn't understood and I had to resort to age-old sign language before I could find out directions to the Plaza. As we walked on I noticed that most of the houses opened onto the street and people were sitting outside their doors on chairs or stools, enjoying the relative coolness of the outside air. These town homes were very colonial-looking: square; single-storied; and mainly consisting of two rooms. I could easily see into the houses. Most of them had dirt floors but a few were concreted, and all were crammed full of beds; cookers; chairs; piles of clothes; children; motorcycles and bicycles.

Most of the contents seemed to be covered with a thin layer of dust and the sheets on the beds were filthy. The people, however, were cleanly dressed and the children looked up at us with shining faces, oblivious of their primitive living conditions.

As we got nearer to the centre of town, we passed numerous railway crossings which had boards at either side. On these boards were lights which flashed continuously, even though the line was completely clear. Here and there, I noticed a few shops, they were like the ones in Mexico City and opened right onto the pavement. Everything inside was stacked in piles or placed behind windowed counters. All the shops had a corrugated iron door in the roof that was pulled down at night to shut the shop.

We eventually reached the main street and, by now, our feet were aching and we were thirsty, so we made our way to the Plaza. Each Mexican city had a plaza or Zocolo which is the meeting place of the town. I was to see many of every size and description while sightseeing in Mexico. There was a fountain in the centre of this plaza and a canteen that sold drinks. We sank down into seats that were arranged in front of the canteen and we were pleased that we had chosen a table with an umbrella over the top, because, when we looked up, we could see that on every inch of telephone or electric wire in the square sat a bird the size of a swallow. There must have been thousands of them sitting there, twittering contentedly and, every now and then, depositing another white stain on the street below!

We felt much refreshed after a short rest and a drink, so we made our way back along the coast road to the ship.

We stayed in Mazanillo for two and a half days loading mainly cotton.

The ship had already been to a number of ports before we joined and the holds contained such cargo as shark's fins; acetic acid; Mexican curios; leather goods; spare parts for cars (originally from Japan to be assembled in Mexico and returned to Japan); rum and seashells. I went ashore again on the second day this time with the Chief Steward's wife, and we had a very interesting wander around the shops. When we arrived, during the morning, the streets were quite crowded and we had difficulty getting past the people selling things on the side of the street. These 'hawkers' were very clever. They stood at the side of the pavement with stacks of woven baskets and brightly coloured hammocks, until you approached. Then they pounced out and started to interest you in their goods. In one place we saw a man trying to sell some small animals which he had tied on a string. They looked like squirrels but were only the size of hamsters. They were sandy coloured with dark lines running down their backs, and they had long bushy tails. They were obviously very frightened and strained to get away from their captor. We gave them a wide berth.

All too soon we were back at sea, making our way out of the harbour entrance, on our way to San Carlos.

CHAPTER 4

SAN CARLOS AND THE COTTON FIELD

During the thirty-two hour passage to San Carlos, the automatic gyro compass stopped working and so the ship had to be steered by hand. At meal breaks, when the helmsman left the bridge, I had a turn at steering. Before I took over Colin said it would feel like driving a car on ice with four flat tyres and I found it was an apt description. The effect of turning the wheel did not take place for quite a time after the action but, if the lock to bring it back on course was kept on too long the ship over-adjusted herself. It was a very good experience for me and I soon got quite used to taking over.

That evening we had to put our clocks back to the time we had originally been on at Guaymas. I had no idea where San Carlos was so, during one of Colin's watches, I had a look at the chart and found out that it is situated in the Bahia de Magela (Bay of Magdela) which was half way up the peninsula of Lower California, Mexico.

When we reached the Bahia de Magela the ship was anchored for the rest of the night. I knew that nearly every port in the world requires that ships entering port take on a pilot who knows all the local hazards, tides and anchorages, and quays. Even if a pilot isn't compulsory most companies insist on using one to aid their Captains and Officers. The San Carlos pilot boarded at 6.00 a.m. the next morning. When we were going alongside, no matter what time of day it was, Colin would go on to the bridge, the second mate would go on the poop deck, to tie up aft and the Mate would go on the fo'scle to tie up forward. Although, while at sea, I would often go on the bridge with Colin, when there was a pilot on board I always kept clear of the bridge for fear of getting in the way.

The sun was just rising over the sand banks and distant rocky hills that surrounded the bay, as we caught our first sight of San Carlos. It certainly did not look a very big place and it materialised into just a quay; a few storage sheds; and about twenty to thirty isolated houses half a mile up a dirt road.

As we came alongside I could see the fishing boats tied up alongside the sheltered quay wall. At one time the boats must have been a very gay sight, multicoloured and jaunty under a new coat of paint, but now the paint was wearing thin and was cracked in places and they looked dejected as they lay waiting for another day's fishing. There was also a naval vessel amongst the fishing boats. It had armed uniformed Mexicans on board and had, apparently, been there for over a year. While we were there the sailors spent most of their time eating and fishing and I never found out its real purpose.

The next day was my birthday and so I was pleased when the ship's agent, Diego, asked if the Chief Steward, his wife and I would like to go with him to the nearest town, Constitution. He had some business to attend to there and, in that time, he told us we could have a look round the town. We all agreed and after lunch we piled into his car. It was an American Cadillac with plush upholstery but it had obviously seen better days and had travelled many thousands of miles. I was beginning to appreciate the vastness of Mexico and Diego said that, because of great distances between towns the Mexicans thought nothing of driving several hundreds of miles in a single day. On the following Sunday he proved his point by spending the whole day travelling to Guaymas to collect his wife and children. The round trip was four hundred miles.

There was no actual road through San Carlos, so, until we turned onto the tarmac road to Constitution, rolls of dust flew up from the back of the car. San Carlos was situated on an island of sand surrounded by mosquito-infested swamps, but after only a few miles, the swamps changed into the now familiar desert scenery: sand; cactus; and rough shrubs. There did seem to be more vegetation in this area, however, than around Guaymas and a group of cattle we saw by the road looked quite fat and healthy. They were the breed of cattle that cowboys ride in the rodeo and had long pieces of flesh hanging from their throats. Their heads were adorned with large curving horns. Diego explained that the cattle roamed around the desert until they were mature, then, they were rounded up into corrals and taken for slaughter. He then went on to tell us a bit about the desert itself and it was very interesting to learn that it belonged to the Government. The people, however, could use part of the land for agriculture if they paid levies for it. Irrigation, however, was strictly controlled and only small areas of the vast desert were actually utilised.

As we got nearer the town we saw several cultivated pieces of land, some of them supporting cotton and others sweet corn. In other places we saw the ground being tilled and irrigated ready for planting. Diego stopped the car at the side of a large area of cotton. He explained that it was the end of the season but a lot of the bushes still held the fluffy white cotton bolls.

He asked if we would like to go and see at close quarters so we left the car and walked across twenty yards or so of soft sandy soil to the edge of the cotton. There were large cracks in the soil and something disappeared into one of the cracks as I walked over it. I was frightened to ask what it was as I'd been warned of both snakes and scorpions. The branches and leaves on the cotton bushes were so dry and brittle that they broke easily. The cotton itself protruded from the burst seed cases or bolls which grew up the branches. There were only a few bolls left on the branches near the roadside but Diego broke some off for us to inspect. The cotton fibres looked and felt like cotton wool and were slightly oily. Hidden amongst the strands were the seeds which were about the size of a pea, brown in colour and very hard. I saw no more creatures and we were soon continuing our journey.

It was thirty miles between the ship and Constitution but the road was very straight and, with the speedometer needle wavering around the 100 kilometres per hour mark, it wasn't long before we arrived. At a road junction, in the centre of town, stood a huge bronze bust of a man. I had seen similar ones in Mansanillo and knew that they were quite common in Mexico to honour the memories of famous people. Diego proudly told us that this one was of his brother's Godfather who had brought business and prosperity to the town of Constitution. After circling the bust several times to make sure we had a good look, Diego continued through the town and then turned right into a sandy track that ran at right angles with the main street. We bounced up the track and came to a halt outside a concrete building which was the cotton exporter's office. We followed Diego into the office and while he started his business, one of his associates showed us samples of cotton that had been taken from each export bale. He showed us how they tested them for quality. The samples were laid out on a table and then brightly lit by a strong strip light. As we looked at the process the man told us that the cotton was graded according to the amount of impurity (pieces of case or seed) left in the fibres. The best quality cotton was worth up to £500 per quarter ton bale and so the grading was very important to the producer.

We left Diego to his business and strolled along the main street. The shops that lined the street were nearly all glass fronted and were much more modern than the ones in Manzanillo. The whole town, however, was very dusty and the windows of the shops were so filthy that you had to get right up close to them to be able to see the displays inside! When we went inside, we found that most of the wares were also covered in a fine film of dust. Before long Diego came to find us and took us to the Post Office which we had been unable to find. I had already noticed how slow and drawn out the Mexican way of life was and that the Mexicans, as well as being generally lethargic were very talkative. Of course, the native language was Spanish in origin and I wasn't surprised that the most commonly used word was 'Manana' (tomorrow, or tomorrow will do!) This attitude had already frustrated the officers back on the ship to get the cargo loaded quickly, but I couldn't help thinking that it was exactly this attitude that gave the Mexicans their charm. They seemed determined to enjoy life, even if it meant letting the world go by around them, and although, at times, they seemed incredibly lethargic by our standards, they did have reserves of energy which, when released, far excelled our expectations. It took me a long time to form a real opinion of the people, and, of course, generalisations are always a bit dubious but, overall, I found them very friendly, happy-go-lucky, unhygienic and crafty. The women I found to be dark-eyed, sensuous, tough and held in high esteem by their menfolk. The men were proud, hot-bloodied, loud-mouthed and protective towards their families and the children were enchanting; always dirty, smiling and mischievous.

At the Post Office we had a perfect experience of the 'Manana' attitude. The agent came in with us and chatted for a while, with the clerk behind the desk. The clerk then took our letters, had another conversation with Diego, this time about England and how he had never sent a letter there before, weighed the letters, put them back on the counter and waited a bit before opening a drawer to reveal sheets of stamps. After sorting through many sheets as though he'd never seen them before, he then put them back and closed the drawer. He then consulted a book to see what charge was made for airmail letters to England. After reading deeply, he finally found the correct charge and went back to his investigations of the sheets of stamps in the drawer. After much adding and subtracting he eventually handed over the correct stamps and we, in turn, handed over the correct money. It still took several minutes to check the money and by the time we actually left the building twenty minutes had elapsed!

When we got outside again Diego suggested that we go for a drink to wash away some of the dust and we readily agreed. He took us to a Hotel near the centre of town. We entered through a gap in a palm fronded wooden wall and came into a beautifully cool looking garden. The floor was only soil and the garden chairs sank into it as we sat on them but after the fierce heat outside it was very refreshing to be surrounded by plants and with a shady awning over our heads.

There were several varieties of trees in the garden, the only ones I recognised were rubber trees. Amongst the trees were cages containing highly coloured birds and some of the squirrel-like animals we'd seen on sale in Manzanillo. Feeling much refreshed after drinking ice-cold coca-cola, we emerged from the garden and got back into Diego's car. We decided that it was now time to return to the ship for the evening meal, so we turned round and left town.

On the way back, we passed a gin plant where the cotton was processed into the quarter ton bales ready for export. Diego said that we could go and visit it if we wanted to so, throwing all cares of food aside, we agreed. Diego went to ask permission for our visit and then led us to the huge processing building. As we entered the massive sliding doors, a wave of noise engulfed us and any conversation was completely overwhelmed. It was quite easy, however, to see what the machines were doing. The raw cotton was brought to the plant by lorry and then sucked through the roof into the machines. The first machine had rattling, vibrating belts running through it and separated the white fluffy fibres from the seeds and cases. These were then redirected elsewhere Diego told us later that the seeds were used to make cattle feed, cotton seed oil and margarine. The cotton fibres that remained were conveyed across heated rollers which had small combs attached to them. The combs pulled the cotton into lengths. Eventually the stretched fibres were fed out in layers, one on top of the other, until a pile had been made. Then presses closed around the pile and pressure was applied. Whilst the pile was under pressure, a group of men wrapped a piece of muslin around the cotton and then, using four or five strands of wire, bound the bale together. After some minutes the presses were switched off and the completed bale, now about three feet high and two feet wide, was taken away to be weighed and marked with an identification number. We emerged from the other end of the gin plant with the noise of the machines still ringing in our ears. I was really pleased that I had had the opportunity to see the plant and even though it had taken us over half an hour, we still got back to the ship in time for the meal!

I knew that it was a custom on ships, when it is your birthday, to stand the cost of the celebration drinks, so in the evening Colin and I invited everyone into the bar. I felt a bit guilty that it was Colin who actually had to pay but one of the Shipping Companies' Superintendants, who was visiting the ship helping with engine repairs, made a donation towards the evening's drinks so Colin's bill was not too shocking! I was grateful, however, that I had been born on 28th and not 29th October like the Third Engineer. It so happened that no cargo was being worked on the 29th and all the engineers knocked off at lunch time. Consequently the celebrations to mark the Third Engineer's birthday started at midday and his bill was £22. At 10p for a beer and 6p per tot for Spirits that was quite a lot of drinks consumed!

We stayed in San Carlos until the following Thursday evening. During that time, as there was nothing to see ashore, I sunbathed and watched various people fishing from the quay. Their efforts were not very well rewarded but some of the stewards caught a few small fish. They tied them on strings and left them in the sun to dry and they were later used to make some Indian 'delicacy'. I asked Colin what kind of food the crew had and he told me that they had curries at every meal, even for breakfast. At first, this fact astonished me but it was not as monotonous as it sounded because besides curried fish and meat they had curried lentils, vegetables, roots etc. and each curry was served with a vast assortment of accompaniments including poppadoms, sultanas, coconut and apples. I was not very fond of curry so our menus interested me far more. They were extremely varied. For breakfast there was a choice of grapefruit, melon, or stewed fruit and then cereals, after which 'eggs to order' would feature. These could be accompanied by different combinations of bacon, sausage, fried bread; liver or potatoes. For lunch was always a soup followed by a main course of maybe Cornish pasty, chops, fish cakes and vegetables or a choice of cold meats and salad. Often there was a choice of curry as well. The sweets varied considerably from sponge puddings, fruit or fritters to pancakes and blancmange and, if the sweet was not to one's liking, there was the choice of biscuits and cheese. The evening meal was equally varied but generally started with melon or fruit juice and soup, followed by an entrée of sweetcorn or stuffed peppers etc., and then followed by a roast meat with vegetables, or about once a week, steak. The sweet generally was ice-cream, with or without fruit and, or, biscuits and cheese. The quality of the food was excellent and often we had such luxuries as oysters, shrimps, and avocado pear. Generally, it was well cooked too, so I had to be very careful not to eat too much. I seldom had breakfast as by cutting out that I could miss one whole meal, but if I could help it, I never missed lunch or the evening meal! It might seem like heaven to most housewives but I really missed cooking and after a few weeks just yearned to be slaving over a hot stove and washing up afterwards.

One day, while we were in San Carlos, a party of school boys visited the ship. They were all very excited and wanted to see everything but they were rather unruly and spread around the ship like wild fire. Colin had been given the job of showing them around, but there were so many of them with only one teacher that they just disappeared in every direction. I think that the only one who went on the guided tour was the teacher. When he had seen enough, over an hour later, his smiling, chattering boys were rounded up and ferried off the ship.

I think that we were all quite pleased when we left San Carlos as there had been so little near to the port. I was told, however, that Ensenada, our next port of call, was a much more interesting place.

CHAPTER 5

ENSENADA AND MY FIRST SHOPPING EXPEDITION

During the thirty-eight hour passage to Ensenada we were lucky enough to see two whales or rather the signs of two whales. One showed itself by blowing water spouts high into the air accompanied by a rushing wind-like grunt. The other was at a far greater distance but we could see that it was leaping right out of the water. When it re-entered it made a huge splash which shot white foam many feet into the air. We also saw a number of dolphins with markings I had not seen before. They had the usual shining purple-black backs but their bellies and throats were white. By now I was getting quite used to taking over the wheel for short periods and I quite enjoyed being of some use to the running of the ship, as, being a supernummery, I always felt insignificant. Any responsibility, no matter how small, was very welcome.

On the eve of our arrival at Ensenada a thick fog rolled in and our speed had to be reduced to half ahead. The fog horn was activated which produced a huge, booming blast every four minutes. It always took me by surprise as the periods of silence were just long enough for you to forget that it was switched on. The fog, which was one of the worst hazards for ships and hated by sailors, remained all night and it wasn't until we approached the harbour of Ensenada itself that it started to lift. By 8.00 a.m. we were alongside.

Ensenada Bay stretched around the horizon for many miles and the town huddled between the hills and mountains and sea. Leading from the town we could see the highway that led to the American border, hugging its way along the base of the mountains in the distance. A number of large yachts were anchored in the bay and, during our stay, several thousand pounds of yacht arrived and left carrying their American owners southwards to the sun. Ensenada was less than a hundred miles from the American border so at weekends, the town was crowded with Americans who arrived not only on yachts but in cars and motorised caravans.

It didn't take long for the Chief Steward's wife and I to arrange a trip up the road and, armed with a pile of letters and a few pesos, we made our way towards the dock gates. There was a high sea wall built alongside the road leading to the gates. Nearly its entire length, about half a mile, was covered with paintings. Each painting was done on the bare wall and was about eight feet by six feet. The Chief Steward's wife, who had been there before, told me that they had all been painted by local schoolchildren. They looked very professional and each depicted a scene relating to the sea. There were pictures of: ships at sea; ships in harbour; burning ships; sailing ships; ships in distress; fish; turtles; mermaids; dolphins; divers; charts and even a King Neptune. Some of the paintings had been signed in the corner and the ages of the children written in brackets beside the signatures. The ages were between eight and twelve years old and I couldn't help thinking how proud Rolf Harris would have been of these youngsters! There were armed guards on the dock gate and although they stared quite hard they didn't stop us. Some mangy dogs lay in the shade around the gatehouse, obviously hoping to pick up some morsel of food at the dock. They were very careful, however, to keep out of the guard's boot range.

As we walked along the side of the highway towards the town, the sun shone warmly on our backs. There were a lot of cars on the highway. They were travelling fast at first but, as they approached the town, they had to slow right down to negotiate the ribs of concrete that had been placed in the road specifically for that purpose. In the town the pavements and shop fronts were cleaner than in Manzanillo but the streets were still dusty and there was an atmosphere of unkemptness . We wandered along the streets and tried to find the Post Office, but my feeble attempts at enquiring its location were either met with complete bewilderment or mild humour and I decided that I would have to work hard at my Spanish pronunciation. In the end we found that many of the shopkeepers spoke English. The shops in this street were 'tourist' shops. Although they were interesting to browse around the prices in them were very inflated and it was far wiser to shop elsewhere. I soon understood how necessary it was to learn the art, for art it was, of shopping in Mexico. There were two basic rules to follow. The number one rule was not to buy in the tourist shops if you could get what you wanted elsewhere, and rule two was to always challenge the price. It was a well-known fact that the salesmen asked more for their goods than they really expected to get so that even the locals had to bargain them down to the correct, reasonable price. I noticed that the American tourists rarely bargained with salesmen and the Mexicans obviously made a fortune from them. At first I found bargaining a bit embarrassing, especially in the shops, but bargaining with hawkers in the street was quite fun, and a real challenge of wits! The method I used, which I learned from experience, was first to offer far less than half the original asking price which left plenty of room to manoeuvre. The first offer always appalled the salesman and made him frown and shake his head. If I said nothing, he would then consider my offer and knock maybe 10% off the original asking price. I would then stick adamantly to my original offer and he would again utterly refuse. Eventually, after repeating the same prices and offers several times I would increase my offer to the level just below what I considered a fair price(in other words a bargain price for me). The salesman was never tempted and always stuck to his price. My final tactic was to start walking away, acting as though I was no longer interested. I found this very difficult to do especially when I really wanted something, but nine times out of ten it worked and the salesman came down to a fair price and I accepted. Occasionally they even accepted my bargain price! This method of shopping was extremely time consuming and I'm very glad it's not the same in England, however, when I got a bargain price it was extremely satisfying.

In the end we found the Post Office. By the time we had posted our letters it was fast approaching lunch time and we decided to return to the ship. The stevedores had started to load cotton straight away and when we arrived back at the quay they were in full swing. The crane jibs moved back and forth carrying the stacked bales of cotton into the holds, where they were manhandled into position and lashed securely.

At all times there had to be at least one Engineering Officer and one Deck Officer on board the ship. When an Officer was due to do such duties he was said to be 'day, or night, on board'. As far as the Deck Department was concerned it was either Colin's or the Second Mate's duty to do the 'days, or nights on board' but that evening the Mate kindly said that he would do Colin's 'night on board' duties for him so both Colin and the Second Mate were able to go ashore. At 8.00 p.m. a whole group of us tumbled down the gangway with a great feeling of freedom. It was a feeling most people on board experienced because of the confinements of the ship and, as far as the Officers were concerned, when they were off the ship they knew that they were really off duty. When they were on the ship they could be called on at any time. One of the lads hailed a truck that was passing the ship and the driver kindly offered, in sign language, to take us to the dock gate. We piled in and rattled and crashed up the quay. We had thought that the bus which had transported us from the airport to Guaymas had been exceptional, but the truck wasn't in much better condition and most of the vehicles we saw in Mexico had at least one dent, scratch or patch of rust showing through a thick layer of dust and dirt!

Our destination that evening was the oldest taverna in Mexico, a place called 'Hussongs' which was on the outskirts of Ensenada. Apparently it had been running since 1892 and it looked as if it had! Sawdust was thrown about on the floor and the paint, what little that was left, was peeling off the wall. The bar stretched the full length of the room, about a hundred feet, and was just like a 'cowboy movie' bar. There were circular tables and old chairs with worn leather seats scattered here and there. The atmosphere of the place, however, was quite magical and the Cuba Libres (Rums and Cokes) which they served up were equally alluring. The walls were adorned with hundreds of sketches of its various customers which had been drawn by a budding local artist and regular customer of the cantina. They were such good characterisations that the faces seemed to jump out of the paper. There were jaunty Mexican ladies; aged American men with bald heads and cigars in their mouths; blue-rinsed American ladies; and long-haired hippy youngsters; which showed just how diverse the clientele was. An armed guard did sentry duty on the door which frightened me a bit but I was assured that it was merely a preventative measure and that there was one on the door of every establishment that sold alcohol. We stayed chatting quite a long time before our party broke up into groups and drifted off to different bars, hotels and night clubs. Colin and I decided that we would go for a walk through the shops and then back to the ship. Some of the shops were still open which we found very surprising as it was after 10 p.m. We returned to the ship along the coast road and we were very glad that we did when we found a stall selling American hamburgers. We bought two and continued our walk happily chomping our way through roll, salad, hamburger steak and chips.

The next day the wind dropped and I decided to spend the whole afternoon looking around the shops. I met the Chief Steward's wife on her way back, laden with souvenirs. It must have been unusual to see a female walking alone in Mexico, as nearly every car hooted or its driver stuck his head out of the window and 'cat called'. At first I found this an ego boost but after a while, it became insulting and quite annoyed me. I was to learn that Mexican men are very hot blooded and showed their affections very openly, however, if other men showed their liking for any of their daughters or wives, blood could flow!

I found the souvenir street without any difficulty and went into nearly every shop along its length. I did enjoy myself. There were so many Mexican curios and goods piled into every shop that the choice was overwhelming. There were leather goods, straw hats, hand woven blankets, silver and abalone shell jewellery, embroidered blouses and dresses, Mexican dolls, pottery, paper mache figures; shells; ponchos; stuffed animals, and postcards. I wandered for two hours in and out of all the shops.

Eventually I came to the river that ran through the town to the sea. It was a good landmark and I remembered it from the day before so I easily re-discovered the Post Office. As I walked along the river bank I noticed that it was almost completely dry and that roads led from one bank to the other. The locals drove their cars right across the river bed not having to bother to go round and find a bridge. After posting another batch of letters which I had collected on board, I walked back down the high street. Here I found a material shop that sold every type and colour of material possible. I was particularly interested in the cotton material. It was a real bargain at 60p a yard.

As Ensenada was to be our last port of call in Mexico this time round, I decided to start buying souvenirs. I had great fun bargaining and when I returned to the ship I was loaded down with a doll dressed in National costume, a T-shirt with Ensenada written on it, a hand embroidered blouse and a picture frame made from cactus wood.

During the afternoon we heard that besides the other cargo we would be taking three passengers with us to Hong Kong. They arrived during the late afternoon and we all introduced ourselves. Two were Swiss lads en route around the world; and the other was a Mexican man on his way to do missionary work in India. It didn't take them long to get settled in and that evening at 7.00 p.m. the engines fired and we were on our way to Japan.

CHAPTER 6

THE FIRST PACIFIC CROSSING AND THE BROKEN TOE

Now that we were away from the coast, we settled into life at sea. Because I had been on a ship before, I knew that shipboard life was totally different from that experienced elsewhere. It had taken me nearly two months on my first trip to get used to such a strange way of life but this time I adjusted quite easily. While at sea, of course, the ship was run on a twenty-four hour basis and I think that in itself was the main reason for life being so different.

Each twenty-four hours was split into two twelve-hour periods which were each sub-divided into three periods called watches, therefore, each watch lasted four hours. Because there were three Mates on the Amparo, each took a four-hour watch with eight hours off in between, thus working eight hours in every twenty-four.

This was also the case in the Engine Room, although there were more than three Engineering Officers the ones not doing watches did 'day work'. Colin as third Mate did the eight to twelve watches, day and night, the Second Mate did the twelve to four and the Mate did the four to eight ones. In the Engine Room the watches were often changed around between different officers. Because the ship was run on such a basis, different people had different routines each centring around watch times. This meant that there was nearly always someone eating, always someone sleeping and always someone working, no matter what time of day it was! Because Colin's watches were from 8.00 a.m. to midday and 8.00 p.m. to midnight, our routine centred around those times and often we would go several days without seeing some of the other officers, on opposite watches, because they ate, slept and worked at totally different times to us.

I had always been a creature of habit and so I found, from the beginning, that I could fit happily into the routine of sea life. When Colin was called at 7.30 a.m. I also got up and, after cleaning the cabin, did any washing and ironing that had accumulated, luckily, however, I did not have to wash the bedding and towels as these were classed as ship's laundry and dealt with by the Laundryman. After washing and ironing I used to stock up the bar fridge and wash up any glasses that had been left from the night before. By that time it was 9.30 a.m. when I went up onto the bridge to see Colin and have a look around. 'Smoko' (a shipboard jargon word for coffee/tea break) was at 10.00 a.m. and I used to return to the cabin to have my cup of coffee. Between coffee time and 11.30 a.m. I disciplined myself to study Spanish from a 'Teach Yourself Spanish' book and to write up my diary. The rest of the morning I spent on the bridge, watching the weather, sea and wildlife.

Lunch was served between midday and 1.00 p.m. and after lunch Colin 'turned in' (shipboard jargon for going to sleep) for the afternoon as he could never get a full night's sleep when doing watches. Sometimes, generally every other day I would 'turn in' too for a couple of hours mainly because there was nothing else to do. I had brought with me knitting, sewing and tapestry and so, after afternoon 'Smoko' at 3.00 p.m. I could keep myself occupied until 5.20 p.m. when I accompanied Colin onto the bridge to do dinner relief for the Mate, and when he returned we had our own dinner.

After dinner we sometimes watched a video tape and at 8.00 p.m. if was time for Colin to go back on watch again. I filled the rest of the evening with sewing and sometimes I went into the bar for a chat with the other Officers. Until 9.30 p.m. when I returned to the bridge to see what was going on and then after reading a book from a well stocked library I would turn in for another day.

On the first day out of Ensenada, even though the swell was not very high and the sea surface unbroken, the ship tossed and gyrated as though she was trying to free herself from some terrible adversity which was clinging grimly beneath her. One minute she was rolling (going from side to side); the next pitching (moving from bow to stern); and the next corkscrewing in a terrifying manner. Luckily, I had never been afflicted by the dreaded sea sickness and I was not on this occasion, however, even a few of the hardened sailors became ill and the three passengers did not even emerge from their cabins for the first two days!

Even though I didn't feel sick, my balance, which wasn't very good even on dry land, proved very tiresome. I was forever bumping into things and after only a few hours I was bruised all over. Eventually I got used to moving with the ship but when the actions were so erratic even that was difficult. Other precautions also became a habit and soon it was second nature to make sure that everything was stowed properly; that cups and glasses were always held on to and that, if I was washing, a bucket was put by the sink to catch the water that slopped out of it.

Because it was necessary, I noticed that the ship was well prepared for bad weather. There were handrails everywhere, even in the showers and in all the corridors. The chairs in the cabins and the saloon could be fixed to the floor and the dining tables had raised edges. Underneath the tablecloths thick blankets were soaked in water and this prevented things from slipping around.

At the end of the second day, the swell calmed down and everything returned more or less to normal and eventually the seamen could go out on deck and start to chip and paint the main deck. During the following days I spent a lot of time watching the sea. It was never boring and I was amazed to see that it could change so quickly from being supremely beautiful to treacherously ugly. The colours of the water were quite bewildering and ranged from black to white through every shade of blue and green imaginable. When there was a slight swell and a gusty wind blowing, the sea broke against the bows of the ship and created a beautiful bow wave which hissed and bubbled along the ship's side turning from deep blue to very pale, clear turquoise. As it moved the length of the ship it mounted into waves, became white and then disappeared into a flurry of fine delicate spray, leaving behind a faint rainbow image. At night the whole performance was often highlighted with phosphorescence, making everything twinkle and sparkle as if lit by a million tiny bulbs from below.

The sky was also very interesting and, because there were no obstacles between ourselves and the horizon I found that I could get a panoramic view of storms or sunsets which I had never experienced on land. I loved watching storms, I could see them approaching from over fifteen miles away. The clouds used to rush together into black smudges and move and expand until they merged into the sea itself. Sheets of rain joined the clouds to the sea and I could then follow their track for many miles. Often it appeared that the approaching rain storm would be coming towards the ship and then it would veer off and disappear over the horizon and I had experienced a whole storm without being affected by it at all.

Every night at dusk I watched the sunset which I knew could be very spectacular but I nearly missed the best one of the passage. Colin and I had arrived on the bridge as usual at 5.30 p.m. to do the dinner relief and we had already missed the sun's descent. The Mate told us that as the sun had disappeared over the horizon it had been highlighted by a splendid green flash. The sky, however was only just beginning to become beautiful. There was a thin layer of auto-cumulus cloud in the sky. It resembled cotton wool that had been pulled apart and laid across the heavens. The cloud was pale grey in its thickest parts but this radiated into silver and its edges were laced with pale rosy pink. All around the horizon the sun had thrown its shadow of colours and delicate shades of pink; mauve; orange and yellow radiated outwards from the area where the sun had disappeared. This silvery-pink column of cloud drifted along in front of the backcloth of colour, the sight was breathtaking. It was a full half an hour before the colours slowly merged back into blues and greys of the sky, but, as if reluctant to disappear altogether, when it was nearly totally dark, the sky around the area where the sun had descended turned into deep orange. The fluffy clouds, now almost black, reflected this beautiful colour along their tattered edges before, eventually, the colours disappeared into the night.

During the crossing there were high winds and rain and the ship, although a lot steadier than on the first two days, rolled and rocked nearly every day. When she occasionally decided to give us a rest, I realised how accustomed I had become to her wild movements and when she was steady I found myself overcorrecting my balance and being in a worse state than when she'd been moving erratically! It was pleasant, however, not to have to hold soup bowls up from the table, tilting them frequently, to prevent their contents from sloshing over the table cloth, and it was much easier to sleep when she was still.

On the third day out of port we were joined by a group of albatross and after that we were accompanied by at least one on every day of our passage. The first to join us were black in colour but later these were joined by the massive Laysan variety. The albatross were very impressive birds. They were about the size of geese, at least their bodies were but they looked so much bigger because of their enormous wing span which in most cases was over ten feet! They had round fluffy heads and short necks which made them look as if they were cold. Because of their far reaching wings they were able to glide along effortlessly in our wake, often not having to flap their wings from one hour to the next. They would swoop down behind the ship and, at times, they were so close to the sea that they were lost from sight behind the waves, but, even though they were so close, they never touched the surface. They seemed to be able to live quite adequately from the scraps that were thrown overboard. To pick up these scraps they had to land on the sea where they would float like ducks on a pond. To regain the air they simply stepped out of the water; ran up a nearby wave; extended their legs sideways like irate turkeys; unfurl their wings and gracefully glide away. They gave me endless entertainment and they were obviously wonderful company for any seaman or woman. Sometimes they would fly above the bridge wings, cock their heads on one side, look me straight in the eye and seem to say' How are you today then?'

While we were passing some thirty miles north of the chain of Sandwich or Hawaiian Islands, we had more bird visitors. These were much smaller than the albatross only about the size of sparrows. They were exhausted and landed on the ship for a rest. They didn't take long to recover, however, and soon flew off again in the direction of nearby islands One, however, was not so fortunate as the rest. After two days' gentle nursing, warmth, food and water he died and was 'buried at sea'. I had seen birds using ships as resting places on our previous trip to sea when we were sailing down the Mexican coast after it had been swept by a hurricane. That time we had been visited by scores of birds that had been thoroughly battered and even had feathers missing, but most of them had survived after being given food and water and we were glad to see them fly off again.

As the days passed the temperature dropped. This meant packing away summer clothes and bringing out winter ones. The Officers changed from their summer uniform of white shorts; white short-sleeved shirts and white socks to dark uniform trousers; long-sleeved shirts and jumpers. I always found it difficult to decide what clothes to take with me, especially when we didn't know our ports of call. I found that the only answer was to take a bit of everything. I had packed as many separates as possible and most of my dresses were pinafores which I could wear with jumpers in the cold places; on their own in hot places and with a blouse in between. The real secret was to have things that could be worn in layers, that is, on their own or with a single or combination of layers according to the temperature.

I had also brought a fair selection of things like talcum powder, aspirins, emery boards and paper handkerchiefs because I wasn't sure that I could get them in every country that I was likely to visit. As it happened I found that every country I visited on the ship did sell all the commodities I had packed although, of course, different brands from the ones I was used to.

Every two days we had to put our watches back one hour and thus gained an extra hour. When we were twelve hours in front of GMT (Greenwich Mean Time) we crossed the International Date Line and lost a whole day. After that we were twelve hours in front of G.M.T. which thoroughly confused me.

As I mentioned before, in the evenings we often watched a video film and we found that on a long sea passage these certainly helped to fill in some of our spare time. The tapes for the video machine were supplied by a firm called Walport Telmar Marine Company who taped television programmes and films and then distributed them to ships. The tapes were fed through a complex video player but shown on a normal television set. Most of the tapes were very entertaining and I could almost imagine that I was back at home as I watched 'the Sweeny' or 'Love Thy Neighbour'. I often used to do my knitting while I watched a film and the lads used to shout at me, saying that the clicking needles sounded like their Mum's at home!

The distance across the Pacific was 5255 miles and we covered nearly 400 miles every day. I was eager to find out how much fuel we used to travel that distance but when I asked one night in the bar it posed quite a discussion. The third engineer, the Sparky and the Lecky put their heads together and after much sweating over a hot calculator, finally produced the figure of 19 gallons per mile! They stressed emphatically, however, that because of the number of variables (specific gravity; size of engines; slip etc) the figure was very approximate, even so I found it quite staggering.

During the fourteen day passage, we only saw one other vessel, a fishing boat. Apparently, however, we did pass ten ships and a number of fishing boats. We were on a busy shipping lane so I was surprised at the small number of sightings but when I began to think about it, and realised the vastness of the ocean and learnt that different currents encouraged ships going in the opposite direction to select different routes, I began to understand. It did, however, tend to underline the feeling of being 'cut off' which was daily becoming more apparent.

We had no radio with us but some of our ship mates had brought theirs with them and on occasion, when reception was good, they were able to pick up the BBC overseas services which had news bulletins on the hour. Often, however, when reception was bad we were completely oblivious to the happenings in the rest of the world. After living in a radio and television age I found this very disconcerting and, as the days passed, I realised that even in the 1970's life at sea was essentially a solitary one.

I realised how completely self-sufficient the ship had to be whilst at sea. And even though this was rather a nice thought connected with wars and household accounts, it became rather a frightening one when connected with emergency services and hospitals.

A few days before our arrival in Japan these deficiencies were brought home rather clearly to us. One morning the third engineer accidently stubbed his little toe against his bunk which resulted in it ending up a sorry mess and sticking out at right angles from the rest of his toes. Of course there was no hospital to rush him to, not even a doctor, and nothing could be done for him except to feed him pain killers and strap up the offending toe.

On November 19th, the day before our expected arrival in Japan, the weather changed dramatically. After numerous days of cloudy gloom, the thermometers shot up to 20 degrees centigrade and the sun shone in a cloudless blue sky. The same morning we heard that Japan was having an exceptionally mild winter.

On 20th November, one day out of Yokohama, there was an air of excitement which everyone seemed to feel whenever we arrived in port, especially after a long trip at sea, and I was very excited as I'd never visited Japan before. That day, surprisingly, went very quickly, and on waking at 7.00 a.m. the next morning, Japan was in sight.

When I went out on deck the sun was shining brilliantly and I was amazed to see so many ships converging on Tokyo Bay. They came from every possible direction. We took on a pilot before 8.00 a.m. and I went back in the cabin to see him board. He was immaculately dressed in black raincoat and trilby shaped hat and he even wore spotlessly clean white gloves! He was escorted to the bridge and soon our course was set for Yokohama Harbour. We had arrived in Japan.

CHAPTER 7

YOKOHAMA AND MY FIRST IMPRESSIONS OF JAPAN

We anchored in Tokyo Bay for about an hour before going alongside. As we swung around the 'pick' (nautical jargon for anchor), I could see a cloud of pollution over Yokohama and the water in the bay was thick and oily. I was amazed, therefore, when the Chief Steward's wife told me that, before Japan had become industrialised, the locals had collected edible seaweed from the very same Bay.

The second pilot came on board just after 10.00 a.m. and we were taken alongside Yokohama's South Pier, the passenger terminal! I was very pleased about this as it was the closest pier to the town. The landing jetty was lined with happy smiling Japanese families obviously enjoying the Sunday afternoon sun. They took photographs as we tied up alongside and it made us all feel famous!

The agent was the first official on board and he brought with him a huge wad of mail. Soon we were completely absorbed in news from home. It was always exciting to get mail when we were so far away from home but as this was the first mail we'd had for five weeks, it was even more welcome.

As soon as it could be arranged the Third Engineer was taken ashore to an International hospital where he learnt that his toe had sustained a compound fracture. During the days since the incident the bone had knit back together and he was told that, consequently, it would have to be re-broken and pinned together in the correct position, he would be in hospital for at least ten days.

No cargo was being worked until the next day but Colin had to do the 'on board' duties. It didn't stop me leaving the ship, however, and after lunch, armed with camera, I went ashore. I was a little apprehensive at first about being on my own but I knew that I would have to get used to it if I wanted to see anything of the countries we were visiting as the Chief Steward's wife was leaving the ship that day to visit her mother in Kobe and probably would not be returning.

My very first impression of Japan was that it was totally in contrast to Mexico. Everywhere was beautifully clean and everything was well kept. Nearly all the cars were free of dents or scratches and their paintwork shone like new. The people were also immaculate. Even the men's socks had creases ironed into them and the women were so highly groomed and expertly dressed that they looked as if they had just stepped from the pages of a fashion magazine. Even the children were a picture of neatness, their faces shone and their clothes were spotless. The most popular garment for women seemed to be separates: pleated skirts and polo-necked jumpers or blouses and jackets. Many of the men wore suits and ties but the younger ones sported smart shirts or pullovers and polo-necked jumpers worn with trousers that were so well pressed they looked just unpacked from new! I was also surprised to see that many of the women wore the traditional kimono. These costumes were highly coloured and patterned but they made their wearers look very demure especially if they also wore the traditional wooden clogs which made them walk with tiny steps. The children's clothes, apart from being so tidy, were also very pretty. They ranged from little suits of velvet to shoulder strapped pinafores. As well as being smart, the Japanese seemed very conscious of cleanliness. Some people even wore face masks in the street to combat pollution and the taxi drivers wore gloves.

The nearest place to the berth, only a stone's throw away, was a building called the Silk Centre. The Centre housed a hotel, a number of shipping and agency offices, a restaurant complex, a tourist information centre, a post office, and a basement shopping arcade. Because it was Sunday the tourist information office and the post office were closed but the shops were open and I wandered in and out of them admiring the beautiful goods they had on sale. I emerged from the Silk Centre after weaving my way through the labyrinth of restaurants on the ground floor. The restaurants didn't advertise their menus in writing but instead displayed plastic models of the dishes in their windows.

Back in the street again I noticed that nearly every road junction, large or small, had a zebra crossing with signal lights both for pedestrians and motorists so it was an easy task to cross the busy main road and join the throng of people entering a nearby park. It was Yamashita Park and it was laid out formally into grass areas and paths with a few fir trees and bushes here and there. Because it was Sunday everyone seemed to be out and about and the park was crowded with happy, chattering Japanese people, strolling, playing with their children and sitting on the grass having picnics. They ate their food with chopsticks and they carried their packed food in ingenious plastic containers like Tupperware boxes but with separate compartments for each different type of food. From the park I could see the harbour and the M.V. Amparo tied up alongside the passenger terminal. I was very worried at first, about wandering too far from the ship but I had a map of the town with me and soon curiosity got the better of me and I set out towards the shopping streets.

I passed another park on the way which was three quarters covered by a huge baseball stadium that was being built. According to the map I had to turn right after passing the stadium and reaching the railway line, but I nearly missed it as I didn't realise the lines were built above street level on concrete platforms. It wasn't until a train came thundering overhead that I realised it was a railway line! A little further on I passed one of the railway stations and as I did so, crowds of people piled down the steps and made their way towards the shops. By following them I soon arrived at Isazachi Shopping Street.

As most Japanese people work six days a week, Sunday was the main shopping day and every street was crowded with people. They all looked very happy in fact I didn't see a miserable face and they all had their families with them making shopping day into a day out. The Isezachi Cho (street) was completely pedestrianised and paved between the shops. I walked down it for several blocks but even then it stretched so far I couldn't see the end. The shops were much more westernised than the ones I had seen in Mexico and all glass fronted. They weren't quite like the shops in England though because most of them didn't have doors at all. They must have been shut up at night like the ones in Mexico with shutters coming from the roof. There were shops of every kind: greengrocers; department stores; tobacconists ;stationers; gift shops; electrical shops; tea shops; take-away food stalls; jewellers; opticians; supermarkets; bakers and many many more. Between then they sold everything imaginable: but, being a tourist, I especially noticed cameras; watches; hand-painted silk articles; basket work; paper-thin china; and cultured pearls.

Two shops absolutely fascinated me. One was a kimono shop. I knew that the kimono was the national costume of Japan and I had seen pictures of people wearing them but I had never seen one close up before. They were, in fact, just large rectangles of materials which had collars and sleeves sewn into them. They resembled full length dressing gowns. The shop keeper, who spoke perfect English, explained to me that it was the way the kimono was worn that made it such a beautiful garment. He explained that it was put on like a dressing gown and then overlapped in front and tied with a wide belt around the waist. This belt was known as the Obi and was tied in a bow at the back. The women tied their bows very fully and decoratively but the men just tied them with great care. Besides the hundreds of kimonos on sale in the shop, there were many decorative accompaniments to go with them including braids, shoes, over jackets and hairpieces.

The cheapest kimono in the shop was a woollen one priced at the equivalent of £16 and the most expensive one was £250! This expensive one, however, was a real work of art. It was made of pure silk and was a subtle pink in colour. Hand painted on the kimono from hem upwards in radiating spirals were perfect and delicate patterns of apple blossom.

The other shop that fascinated me was a toyshop. It specialised in cuddly toys and was packed to overflowing with them, so much so that there were cuddly toys stacked up outside on the pavement. They ranged in design from huge soft cuddly lions six feet tall to little fluffy dogs that were clockwork and walked about wagging their tails. Needless to say this shop was surrounded with bright-eyed children and reluctant parents!

As I walked back up the street, I noticed that the take away shops and ice cream parlours were crowded and long queues stretched back from them into the street. The Japanese seemed to like Sunday afternoon snacks and hundreds of them chomped their way through hamburgers, chips and Japanese delicacies.

At the top of the street, I passed a fruit shop. It was also open on to the street and I could see its contents easily. The most luscious displays of fruit that I had ever seen were laid out on the counters. Each piece of fruit was placed in containers like egg cartons and seemed to glow with freshness. Most of the fruits were familiar: bananas, oranges, grapes, pineapples, melons, cherries, tomatoes, apples and pears but there were also some fruits not familiar to me. Later I discovered the names of two of the unfamiliar ones, they were lychees; small brown-coated fruits with centres like grapes; and cackis, orange tomato-shaped fruits that tasted like pears.

Just by wandering around the shops I learnt a lot about Japanese people and again I noticed how conscious they were of cleanliness and how much care they took with all their possessions. The shopkeepers wandered around the shops tidying the displays and dusting their goods with feather dusters. When a customer purchased an item it was wrapped with infinite care. Paper bags were seldom used as the shop keepers much preferred to wrap goods in sheets of pretty paper and even such everyday items as sellotape and paper handkerchiefs ended up looking like Christmas presents! I was also very interested to see that instead of using shopping bags most people carried round large squares of material. These they cleverly folded around their purchases and then by tying the corners together made a handle for carrying.

I walked back to the ship by the Town Hall. There were boxes of chrysanthemums set out in the car park which stretched the whole length of the building. There must have been near to a thousand boxes in all and the blooms in them were perfect, their colours ranging from deep russet, through pale purple to sunshine yellow. Already I was beginning to appreciate the Japanese people's love for beauty and perfection and their recognition of those two things in flowers.

To get back to the main road I had to walk through the park that had been so reduced by the huge basketball bowl. There was an open air pop concert taking place in the centre of the park in a large walled auditorium and teenagers peered over the top of the wall to catch a glimpse of the performers. There was no need to buy tickets to hear the music as it was plainly audible two blocks away. By the time I regained the main road I was feeling very weary and so I headed for 'home' and a quiet evening on board ship.

Three gangs of stevedores arrived the next morning and started discharging the Yokohama cargo into barges. I spent most of the morning replying to the letters we had received and I ventured ashore again in the afternoon to post them. Afterwards I managed to find China Town and wandered around amongst the narrow streets crammed with open-fronted shops and seedy looking restaurants. It was certainly a contrast to the rest of the town and some rather strange smells emanated from some of the houses. It was very interesting, however, looking at all the Chinese goods on sale: the willow pattern china; silk pyjamas; and painted eggs amongst the assortment of Japanese souvenirs that I had seen elsewhere. There were several bars amongst the shops and I learnt later that some of the lads had had a good time in them the night before.

Each of the streets seemed to be full of the hustle and bustle that I had always associated with the Orient, although there were certainly far fewer people around than there had been the day before. There were brightly coloured banners wrapped around each electricity pole in the main street and each banner was adorned with writing. I could not decide whether the writing was in Chinese or Japanese but it ran down the length of the banners and obviously advertised the nearby shops and restaurants. The streets at the perimeter of China Town had huge 'gates' built over them. They were in fact more like goalposts than gates with two thick horizontal posts positioned either side of the road with a huge upturned cross piece straddled between the uprights. The gates were highly carved and painted in bright colours. Most of them had only Oriental writing on them but one, the largest of them all, had CHINA TOWN in large letters painted across the centres of the crosspiece.

I had heard that there was a silk museum at the Silk Centre and so after

I had wandered along every street in China Town and taken some photographs I made my way back to visit the museum.

The museum was extremely interesting. It was on the second floor of the Silk Centre and I had to pay to get in. It was very well laid out and showed the complete life cycle of the silk worm, the farming process called sericulture, the method of spinning the silk from the cocoon, the weaving and dyeing processes and several kimonos made from the resulting silk.

There were also many historical details recorded and I learnt that the peak of the silk trade in Japan was around 1940 when 40% of all Japan's exports were silk. The boom, however did not last long and I was surprised to read that for the last few years the only silk exported in large quantities was in the form of scarves.

The life cycle of the silk worm was explained clearly with the aid of diagrams and models. They showed that an egg from the silk worm developed into a larvae which fed on mulberry leaves. The mulberry bushes were grown commercially and the leaves, after being harvested by machines, were taken into a controlled environment and fed to the larvae. When the larvae reached about the length of two inches they are ready to start spinning their cocoons. Square boxes are then put alongside the branches of mulberry and the larvae happily climb inside them and spin their cocoons of silk. The models showed that after several days, the larvae change into a pupae and then left the cocoons as fully fledged moths. There was also a layout showing how to obtain the silk from the cocoons by picking up the end of the thread and unwinding it onto a bobbin. It was then used to weave into silk material.

The display next to the life cycle stand showed many lengths of silk all different in the way they had been woven. There were more than thirty different types on display ranging from satin silk to taffeta silk. There were also different methods of dyeing explained and it stated that the most popular method at that time was the screen printing method although several of the other patterning and dyeing methods were more complex and involved painting wax patterns onto the material to repel the dye in those parts or repeatedly dyeing small parts one at a time with different colours. Of course, there were also diagrams showing artists painting the silk by hand.

The kimonos were displayed upstairs in an Exhibition H. They were all ceremonial ones and very brightly coloured and bold embroidered with silk thread. Above one of the kimonos a poster stated that it took the silk from 10,000 cocoons to make just one of the kimonos and that if the thread obtained was measured from end to end it would reach 1200 kilometres! I suddenly realised why the kimonos were so expensive. When I left the museum I noticed that the Tourist Information Office was open so I went in and collected some very useful information booklets about Kobe, Osaka and also trips to Tokyo and Mt Fujiyama. Then I returned happily to the ship.

CHAPTER 8

YOKKACHI, NAGOYA AND THE TAXI RIDE

We left Yokohama that evening at 7 p.m. and by the next morning at 9.00 a.m. we were taking on the pilot at Nagoya. He took us alongside quay number nineteen. Although the sun was shining there was a distinct chill in the air and later we had very heavy rain which stopped cargo work for a while. I was amazed by the enthusiasm for work. Within minutes of tying up the men started moving the cargo from the holds onto the dock where forklift trucks, working in relay, collected the bales of cotton. They used the forks of the trucks as expertly as using their own hands and wove in and out collecting the bales one at a time. The bales were lifted from the holds by ten ropes attached to a cradle which was rigged to a derrick (on board crane). Each rope had two hooks on it so that when tightened the hooks dug in. Ten bales, weighing two and a half tons, were lifted at a time and swung from the holds in this way.

Each stevadore wore a green crash helmet. His rank was denoted by bands of red painted around the hat. The leader of the gang had three bands painted on his hat, whereas the normal workers had no bands at all. As I stood watching the flurry of activity, a Japanese man came on board and tied three white flags bearing green crosses onto steps and railings. I couldn't think what they signified but I was told later that it was to remind the workers to be safety conscious.

After lunch Colin and I went up the road. We had no idea how far it was to the town but the watchkeeper showed us which direction to take. There were no pavements to the dock road so we had to keep well into the side of the road as a constant stream of cars and lorries passed us. They were transporting goods to and from the various quays and judging from the number of them Nagoya's export figures must have been enormous. The port was surrounded by industrial complexes and I learned from the pilot book that Nagoya was the largest producer of porcelain in Japan. It seemed, however, that every imaginable manufacturing industry had a factory in the vicinity.

We walked for about a quarter of an hour before meeting the main road which led across two bridges towards Nagoya Port town centre. We discovered that Nagoya itself was several miles away inland. We passed rows of small shanty-type houses many of which were built of sheets of rusty corrugated iron. Compared to Yokohama, Nagoya Port was very dirty and unkempt and I began to wonder if my first impression of Japan had been correct. The people, however, were all well dressed and tidy and I realised that it was unfair to compare industrialised Nagoya Port with Yokohama, after all it was like comparing Avonmouth with Bristol!

As we crossed the second bridge we could see the start of the shops. Soon we came to the main street. There weren't many shops however, and no sights to look at so we just wandered aimlessly towards the end of the street. Right at the end we found a subway station that had a single sign outside showing the transport available to Nagoya. It was all written in Japanese so we decided not to venture further as we had no idea where Nagoya was!

A large group of junior schoolchildren passed us as we stood staring at the sign. They were on their way to the station. There was only one teacher with them but she made sure that she could be heard above the chattering of the children by using a megaphone! The children noticed immediately that we were foreigners and chattered even more excitedly amongst themselves. As they passed by many of them smiled and shouted 'bye bye' and waved. They weren't wearing uniforms but they all wore bright yellow hats so that they could be recognised easily.

As we wandered back up the street we saw a number of Pachinko houses. The game of Pachinko seemed so popular in Japan, it was almost an institution. Every shopping street had one Pachinko house. We could see that inside were rows and rows of machines. They looked a bit like pinball machines set up on one end. Later in the trip I went inside a Pachinko house to see how it worked. It was mainly a game of luck but some skill was involved. All the machines were the same in principle but from house to house the method of operating the machines differed. On the machines that I used the player brought a number of small silver balls for 10 yen which automatically appeared at the bottom of the screen. You had to propel the balls, one at a time, to the top of the machine by flicking a spring loaded handle. The balls descended rapidly, because of gravity, through a course of nails and obstacles attached to the back of the screen. At the bottom of the machine there were rows of holes into which the balls dropped. Each hole was numbered and lights lit on a scoreboard marked in a square. If the player lit up a row of lights or four in the centre he got a specified amount of coins back from the bottom of the machine. These coins could then be fed back into the machine, as they were 90 times out of 100 cases, or traded in for prizes. The luck element of the games was created by the effects of gravity, the skill part was how hard you let the spring hit the balls. Some machines I saw added refinements like gates. If the balls went into a gate, they were returned to the pool to be used again. Other machines had hatches that dropped down if you hit a certain number. If you could then get a ball in the hatch you got a free play. Some of the older machines didn't take coins but worked by using balls in the top of the machine. The balls could be bought from or sold to an attendant.

It was quite fun to play a few games of Pachinko but I couldn't understand its massive popularity. In some towns there were whole streets of Pachinko houses and each house had more than a hundred machines. However, no matter what time of day or night it was they were in use and on shopping days we often saw queues outside the houses!

The Amparo was due to sail from Nagoya the next evening but when we got back we heard that there was a delay because of engine trouble. One of the seven pistons in the engine had needed to be dismantled as it had been making rather a lot of strange noises during our Pacific crossing. Unfortunately, however, the piston had seized inside the con rod (piston shaft) and despite the combined efforts of all the engineers over many hours, it could not be removed. The spare piston which the ship normally carried, had already been sent to Kobe for repairs and so a new piston had to be hurriedly ordered. It was delivered to the ship the following day at 1 p.m. and even then the problem of getting it from the quay to the engine room had to be solved. The ship carried no equipment on the after end for lifting such a heavy object and it was no good bringing it aboard the foredeck as there was no entrance to the Engine room from there. The piston was about six feet long and weighed several tons and the only way to get it aboard was to use the stores derrick. It was brought aboard inches at a time. Any moment it was expected that something would part and the piston would go crashing back to the quay. Eventually, however, it stood on the poop deck. Then there was the problem of getting it into the Engine room and into place. A combination of winches and ropes had to be used. For that part of the operation and it was finally put in place at about 10.30 p.m. that night.

I kept well out of the way of the operations as I had been warned that the air was blue! The day's efforts left the engineers tired and with jagged nerves, so luckily for them we didn't sail until 6.00 a.m. the next morning. It was only a two hour passage and by breakfast time we had arrived at Yokachi.

I saw from the chart that it was a long way from the dock to the town and when the Chief Steward said that he had to go back to Nagoya on business and would I like to go with him for the ride, I jumped at the opportunity. A taxi was duly ordered and we set off. We had a little difficulty with the Immigration Officials at the gate which took a fair time to sort out. Eventually our passes were stamped with 'Nagoya' as well as 'Yokachi' and we set off again. After passing through Yokachi we joined a six lane highway and we were immediately held up in traffic. I had never seen so much traffic. The vehicles in all the lanes were nose to tail and sixty per cent of the traffic was lorries. This first hold-up was caused by roadworks but every time there was a lane restriction or traffic lights the traffic built up immediately into miles of tailback. When we eventually reached the roadworks we could see that the workmen were rebuilding the central reservation. Instead of using pre-moulded sections of concrete, however, a complicated mould had been made of wood and placed around the site of the reservation. Concrete was being poured from a mixer lorry into the mould. At both ends of the roadworks there were policemen waving big yellow flags in an effort to keep the traffic flowing.

After passing the roadworks I noticed in the distance, scores of balloons suspended high above a street. The taxi driver couldn't speak English so I had to just guess their purpose. We decided between us that they were an advertising gimmick or to celebrate some special event. As we travelled on amongst the streams of traffic, I realised that we were never going to emerge into countryside. One built up area ran into the next and during the whole journey the largest area of land without building on it was about two acres! Every little piece of land there was used. Even narrow strips between the houses were filled with rice and vegetables. The rice was planted in paddy fields surrounded by banks of earth, holding the water in place. The vegetable plots were neatly planted with rows of vegetables and resembled allotments. The vegetables appeared to be very similar to those we have at home and I recognised, onions, cabbage, cauliflowers, carrots, lettuce, and spinach although no potatoes. There were also many parsnips, larger than ours, hanging on strings to dry. After crossing two bridges spanning estuaries I saw a large amusement park. Most of it appeared to be under cover in a huge glass building, but outside there were rockets and various models to climb on. Nearly every house we passed had at least one blanket hanging from the window and many blankets, sheets, mattresses, and even clothes were hanging out or draped over fences. I thought that it must be washing day but then I realised that as it was a warm sunny day, the bedding and clothes were put out simply to air. It was only thirty miles between Yokachi and Nagoya, but, because of the traffic, it took two hours to get there. Our stay didn't take long, however, and we were soon back amongst the streams of vehicles on our return to the ship. It took us even longer to get back and we didn't arrive alongside the ship until well past dinner time. I had really enjoyed the experience, although I was glad I didn't have to contribute towards the taxi fare of £35!

The stevedores were still working busily when we got back. They were only using single ropes which they fixed round each bale but they were still able to discharge eight bales at one time! The bales were dumped unceremoniously on the quay, where they were stacked into blocks and fork lift trucks carried them into the warehouses. This unloading method was slightly slower and more labour intensive than the one employed at Nagoya but even so by 4.00 p.m. the relevant cargo was discharged and we sailed at 6.00 p.m.

CHAPTER 9

KYOTO AND ITS BEAUTIFUL BUILDINGS

We were called at 7.30 a.m. next morning and Colin went up on the bridge to see us alongside. I went onto the poop deck. The weather had changed quite dramatically and it was much colder and felt frosty. My breath showed up white against the cold air and I hurried back in to don coat and gloves. I read in the local paper later that it was Kobe's first frost of the year but there was snow on the mountain tops in the distance. The pilot and two tugs combined in taking us alongside the Mitsui pier, one of the closest to town and as soon as we tied up stevedores boarded the ship. It had been decided that we would work twenty-four hours a day to get the cargo discharge finished before the Sunday so that we could sail on Saturday night instead of Monday midday. Everyone was disappointed as we were hoping to have two days and nights alongside. Colin and the Second Mate had decided to cover the cargo watches by working six hours on six hours off so it was impossible for Colin to get ashore. I was pleased, therefore, when the three passengers said that I could go with them to Kyoto, the ancient capital of Japan. We were quite an International party: Swiss; Mexican; and English and I was quite glad that the common language was English! We left the ship as soon as our shore passes arrived on board and headed for Sannimijo Station.

There are three types of railway in Japan with most routes covered by all three. The least expensive, and in many cases, the slowest are the private railways. The other two Japanese railway systems are run by the Japanese National Railway. (JNR), one carrying express trains, the other the famous speed 'bullet' trains which reach speeds of over 100 miles an hour but which are extremely expensive to travel on. To get to Kyoto we chose the private Hankyo line and our fare for the one and a half hour journey was only 70p! The 'bullet' train did the same journey in 30 minutes but cost over £5. We were able to identify the individual stations as we passed through them because the signs were written in English as well as Japanese. We were just settling down for the journey, however, when the train stopped at the second station Rokko, and we all had to get out! For some reason the train we had chosen didn't go any further so we had to get off and wait for the next one. We thought that we had to change again in Osaka but an elderly Japanese lady kindly explained in sign language and using our maps to point to, that we had to change before at a place called Juro. This we did and we were soon on the direct train to Kyoto. Most of the seats were occupied but we managed to find some scattered about throughout the carriage. One of the Swiss boys sat next to a Japanese-looking girl who was reading an English book. We started talking with her and it turned out that she wasn't Japanese at all but that she had been born in America. We were a bit embarrassed about thinking her Japanese but she wasn't a bit worried. We told her about our travels and she explained how she was learning to fit into the Japanese way of life. I was very interested when she told us that she was on her way to classes at a special school that taught the ancient Tea Ceremonies. She explained that the Ceremonies were traditional and that most Japanese women knew a few of them. They were all pretty complicated and some took many hours to complete. She also told us that every woman planning to marry in Japan went to special lessons where besides the Tea Ceremonies she learns cookery and flower arrangement. There were many questions I would have liked to ask her but soon she had to get off and we waved her goodbye. As we travelled on I noticed that the surroundings were similar to those around Nagoya and Yocachi with every tiny piece of land utilised. I saw several orchards as well as vegetable patches and paddy fields and some cultivated mulberry bushes.

As we crossed the island, there were fewer and fewer factories and industrial complexes, but just as many houses. I presumed that most of the industry was near the coast so that the raw materials, most of which are imported, are near at hand. Before long we arrived at the end of the line and Kyoto. We had to walk up several flights of stairs to street level and as we emerged into sunlight again, I was surprised to see that Kyoto was a big modern city. According to the tourist map that we had with us, the ancient buildings were dotted around here and there throughout the town. There were so many historic buildings and places of interest it was impossible to contemplate visiting them all so we worked out a route to the temples, shrines and palaces which seemed most interesting to us and after much discussion and enquiry we found the right bus to take us to our first destination, Heian Shrine. The grounds of the Shrine were completely surrounded by a high wall and we had to walk around three sides of the wall to find the entrance which was a large gatehouse. It was very ornate and had two stories however most of the lower storey was cut away to allow visitors to walk underneath. All around the gatehouse there was a walkway which was covered by a turned-up tiled roof held in place by huge round pillars. On looking up I could see a mass of intricately carved waves under the roof. The top floor also had a walkway running around it but this was effectively covered by the curved-edge roof that sat atop the gatehouse like a large hat. The main part of the building was painted white but the pillars, eaves and balconies were vermillion red.

Once past the gatehouse we could see the Shrine itself on the opposite side of a large gravelled area. As we walked towards it, along with scores of other visitors, we stopped now and then to take photographs of the impressive building. It was in the same style as the gatehouse but much larger and even more decorative. On either side, separating the Shrine from the gardens, were twin red and white buildings. The guide map informed us that the Shrine had been built in 1895 to commemorate the 1,100th Anniversary of the founding of Kyoto and that most of its buildings were modelled on a reduced scale after the first Imperial Palace built in AD794. We weren't able to enter Heian Shrine as we weren't practising Buddhists but we could approach the building up a flight of stairs and from that vantage point we could see the ceremony that was taking place inside. A white-robed priest, who had a large scroll, was chanting and waving tiny silver bells over the heads of a row of small boys dressed in brightly coloured kimonos. The ceremony was obviously a form of blessing but as we couldn't understand the language we were unable to tell exactly what was going on.

At either side of the Shrine and in prominent positions around the gravelled area, were a number of trees and bushes on which had been tied 'prayer papers.' These papers which had prayers written on them, could be bought from an attendant and ceremoniously tied to the branches of the trees and bushes. Along the patio of the right hand building that flanked the Shrine there were bowls of flowers for decoration. On closer inspection I discovered that they were tiny chrysanthemums grafted onto bonsai trees. The blooms were only the size of small buttons, in delicate shades of purple, pink and yellow.

After we had feasted our eyes on the beautiful architecture of the buildings, we entered the gardens. One of the passengers was able to explain to me that the gardens of Japanese temples and shrines are designed and planted especially to create a tranquil atmosphere for the visitor. The designers of these gardens certainly succeeded in their aim as far as I was concerned and as soon as I entered, I felt cool and oddly at peace. A pathway led through the trees, the branches of which spread outwards so far that they had to be held up with bamboo frames. Here and there small ponds fed by babbling streams glistened as the sun penetrated the tiny gaps in the umbrella of fir branches. As we walked on the ponds became larger and evergreen trees interspersed the firs. The leaves on the deciduous trees were just changing to their autumn colours of russet, brown and yellow.

Eventually the water from all the ponds flowed into a large still lake. I stopped at the edge and looked down into the clear depths to discover that it was well stocked with Koi fish. The Koi are very famous in Japan and look like very large goldfish, some are even several feet long. Their gold, orange and silver scales glistened in the sunlight. Looking up and into the distance the reflection of the trees, bridges, and buildings merged into the lake and I felt almost spellbound by the beauty and tranquillity of it all. The other visitors seemed to feel the same. Few people spoke and the silence was only broken by the click of camera shutters as we tried to capture the beauty onto film.

The lake had a covered wooden bridge across the centre of it which we had to cross to get back to the Shrine. A lot of people were waiting near the exit gateway as if reluctant to leave and we felt the same way, however, we had lingered for over an hour and we knew that if we didn't hurry we would miss seeing many other buildings.

On the way back to the Gatehouse a group of uniformed school children asked us if we would speak English with them. We readily agreed as we had already been helped by a number of kind Japanese people and we were happy to repay the kindnesses in any way possible. The children asked us where we came from; how long we were staying in Japan; did we like Japan and had we tried Japanese food and they laughed and smiled as we answered them.

We had a lot of difficulty finding our next mode of transport and after asking both bus drivers and tram drivers if they were going near to our next destination and receiving negative answers we took a taxi to prevent any further delay.

Our next stop was Kinkaku-ji temple and as we travelled alone in the taxi we consulted our guide map. It stated that Kinkaku-ji temple (Gold Pavilion) was originally the mountain villa of an Asikaga Shogun, a generalissimo of the Murmachi period (1336-1573). After his death it was converted into a temple. The gold-foiled pavilion with a beautifully laid out garden, is an exact replica, completed in 1955, reviving the grandeur of the original building which had stood for over 550 years until it was destroyed by fire in 1950.

The taxi pulled up in a car park which had several tour buses, and other taxis in it and we left hurriedly to avoid wasting any visiting time. We entered the gardens which this time completely surrounded the temple and again I noticed the tranquil atmosphere that they created. It so overwhelmed us that we were not prepared for the sight which met our eyes as we emerged from the trees. There, on the far bank of a still deep pond, was the magnificent golden temple. It shone in the afternoon sunlight and its reflection was a perfect mirror image in the pond. The sight was breathtaking.

On referring to a pamphlet which had been handed to us earlier, I was able to see that the building consisted of three types of architecture, a different type used for each of the floors. The foundations of the building were of rock raised from the lake bed and at one side a roofed jetty jutted out into the lake. The first floor was built in the palace style of the Fujiwara period and was not gold painted but just plain dark wood. The second story had a fenced balcony running around it covered by a thatched roof with the classical turned up edges. Its eaves and supports consisted of symmetrically carved beams which peeped out under the roof like lace frills. This story was fashioned in the Samurai house style of Kamakura times. It was larger than the first floor, its excess being held up by pillars sunk into the foundations and its gold walls still twinkled in the sunlight except where large square openings gave access to the interior. The third story, in the Karayo (Chinese style or Zen temple style) was much smaller and sat in the middle of the second story roof. Set in the gold painted walls, were oval windows like big eyes and four sets of double doors. The balcony that ran around this floor was more ornate with rounded corner posts like banister posts. On top of the whole building was a final curved roct held up by delicately carved eaves, thatched with shingles and topped by a splendid gold phoenix.

We weren't allowed inside the temple but we spent a long time looking at the outside of the splendid building until a quick glance at our watches forced us on through the gardens to see Kyoko-chi (the mirror pond) which was perfectly round and as its name indicated gave an absolute mirror reflection of the surrounding gardens. We passed by a little wooden tea ceremony house, where, according to the pamphlet Emperor Gominoo drank tea in the olden days, and a small Fudo-do Shrine which contained an imposing stone Buddha as guardian. I noticed that many of the visitors were buying incense sticks and candles which they lit and placed in front of the Shrine on metal stands as offerings.

As we made our way to the next place of interest on our list I read the rest of the pamphlet. It explained the five basic precepts of Buddhism and read:

I undertake the precept from taking life
I undertake the precept not to take what has not been given to me
I undertake the precept to abstain from sexual misconduct
I undertake the precept not to tell a lie
I undertake the precept to abstain from intoxicating liquor.

Our next stop was Toji temple. There were a number of buildings in the vicinity of the temple itself and on walking through the huge covered entrance gate, I felt like I was walking back in time. The buildings were far plainer than at the previous two shrines and made of dark wood but they had fine carvings in the roofs and huge decorative bells hung here and there. In two places there were small covered structures which had fountains in the middle of a large trough. Resting alongside the fountains were large ladles and before they entered, Buddhist visitors washed their hands using ladles full of water from the fountains.

I wasn't sure whether we were supposed to go inside the temple but one of my colleagues decided to go in and came back with descriptions of time honoured art objects and huge Buddhas. I spent our short amount of time at Toji temple, looking at the architecture. Several of the buildings within the temple grounds were grouped around courtyards and guarded by huge ornate wooden gates. There was only one very small garden, most of the grounds being open and gravel covered and I felt that the absence of gardens took away a lot of beauty and the peaceful atmosphere we'd experienced elsewhere, was totally missing.

In one of the corners of the grounds, behind a small shrine, there was a very tall pagoda which had the characteristic sloping roofs on each floor and decorated spire structure on the top most roof. The guide explained that it was the tallest pagoda in Japan and that it was one hundred and eighty four feet high. The Toji temple and its surrounding buildings were founded in 796AD although most of them had been destroyed by the inevitable fires and reconstructed in 1641. I learnt later that they had only narrowly missed being destroyed a second time during World War II but because of the treasures they contained Kyoto and Nara were spared by the American bombers. I was certainly glad about that!

By this time it was starting to get dark so we rushed to get a taxi and visit one more place. We all decided that it should be Nishi Hoganji temple, as it was very near the railway station where we could catch a train back to Kobe.

Again I consulted the guide map. It said that the Nishi Hoganji temple had been founded in 1272 at a place called Higashiyama before being moved to its present site in 1591. It was apparently revered by adherents to

Jodo-Shinsku, one of the largest Buddhist denominations in Japan.

The buildings were again contained within walled grounds and had to be entered through another imposing set of gates. They were made up of four inch thick solid wood and it would have taken several men just to open them! The main temple stood before us as we entered and we were delighted when we realised that there were no restrictions on entry to the building itself. We slipped off our shoes in true Japanese style and entered. From outside the building had looked large but inside it was cavernous! The dark wood walls were solid and undecorated and the temple was in semi-darkness as there were no windows or artificial lights The floor was completely covered with padded bamboo mats called tatamis which were soft to walk on but a bit slippery. Huge metal screens on wheels ran alongside the whole length of the building but in one place they had been drawn apart to reveal an altar bedecked with gold Buddhas and images, flowers and candles. Behind the largest Buddha was a gold cupboard which housed the most valuable treasures of the temple.

The sun had set and it was nearly dark as we emerged once more into the open. Two visitors were putting their shoes back on as we got to the bottom of the steps and I ventured a 'hello'. They answered jovially in American accents and we soon fell into conversation. They told us that they had decided that while they were young they would see some of the world. They had sold up all their belongings and purchased a Pan Am Around the World air ticket for 2400 US dollars and set off. They explained that the ticket entitled them to fly to any country in the world. They weren't allowed to double back on their path but besides that, there were no restrictions.

Japan was their first stop but they planned to visit as many countries as possible. For accommodation they used the cheapest hotels and hostels and they told us of one small hotel in Kyoto where they were being treated as Japanese and when we showed interest they enthusiastically described their room to us. Apparently it was bare of any decoration and contained simply a mattress on a raised dais and a small table which was so low they had to sit on the ground to eat from it. There was no heating in the room except a small burner which was placed under the table. They said it was all that they needed as when they sat round the table they placed a blanket around their knees which kept the warm air next to their bodies.

We didn't part until we reached the railway station but even then we kept finding things to say to each other. It was very satisfying that six people from four different countries could so enjoy chatting to each other. Eventually, after each wishing the other a pleasant journey, we left them and made our way to the station. We had decided to return by the relatively quicker J.N.R. express service and eventually we found the right ticket office. The ticket clerk couldn't speak English and was a bit confused by our sign language but, eventually, after showing him the maps and repeating Kobe several times he understood and issued us with 600 yen tickets. The direct train to Kobe wasn't due for another three quarters of an hour, so my colleagues decided to have something to eat. I was sorely tempted to join them but somehow I couldn't work up any enthusiasm about Japanese food. I wandered around for a while and then rejoined them in the restaurant. They were still in the middle of their meal. One of the Swiss boys had a plate of rice which had little pieces of meat and vegetables in it. The other Swiss boy had rice with a savoury meat sauce and the Mexican had noodles floating in a sea of brown liquid, and accompanied by pieces of fatty meat. None of it looked very appetising to me but they ate it with relish. The Mexican was having great difficulty eating the noodles with the chop sticks provided. The waitress couldn't help laughing when she saw him winding the noodles around the chopsticks but was kind enough to give him a spoon instead. I had a hard time dragging them away from the restaurant and consequently we nearly missed our train. Luckily there were a lot of people to get on and we just caught it and soon we were speeding away from Kyoto.

When I got back to the ship I was still excited about the things we had seen. I had really enjoyed my day out and knew that I would never forget Kyoto.

CHAPTER 10

KOBE AND A ROUGH NIGHT

The next day our sailing time was advanced from early evening to 2.00 p.m. The board on the gangway showed that shore leave ended at 12.00 noon so I went ashore as soon as I could. As I went on deck I passed the Japanese watchkeeper employed by the company to check people boarding and leaving the ship. I learnt quite a lot of things about the Japanese from the watchkeepers in different ports and they were always willing to have a chat. It was from the Kobe watchkeeper that I learnt how the Japanese greeted and addressed each other. On meeting they bow deeply and quickly. The men, when they bow, put their hands on their thighs whereas the women hold their hands together in front of them.

I don't know if they actually did but they always seemed to close their eyes at the same time. The whole action of bowing was solemn and humble. The polite way of addressing other Japanese people was to say their name and then add 'san' afterwards. For example the Kobe agent was addressed as Yuli-san. When addressing someone of higher social standing 'smam' was used after the name instead of 'san'. I found both customs very endearing and I was quite disappointed to hear that, like handshaking in England, these customs were dying out. I also managed to pick up a few Japanese words from the watchkeeper. I learnt that 'arigato' was thank you and 'dozo' was please. That yes was 'hai' and no 'li-e' and 'wakarimasen' was I don't understand. I also noticed the widespread use of the word 'neh' by the Japanese. There is no English equivalent but it is always said as if it was followed by a question mark and literally means, is that so? The Japanese use it in nearly every sentence.

That morning after leaving the ship, I made straight for the Post Office and went through the process of mailing foreign letters. Firstly I had to get the letters weighed at the counter marked foreign mail, and then go to another counter to get the relevant stamps. After that I had to take the letters back to the original counter to have them franked before I could put them in the post box.

The shops didn't open until 10.00 a.m., so I spent the time in between, looking for the shopping streets. I had a map which had been supplied by the Local Seaman's Mission so it wasn't very difficult. On the way to Sannimijo Street, I passed the Town Hall. It had a large flower clock outside but on closer inspection I noticed that it wasn't planted with flowers, as it was so late in the season. Instead, the ingenious Japanese gardeners had used decorative cabbages!

Sannimijo shopping street was completely deserted and the shops had their steel shutters pulled down so I went to what the lads called 'underneath the arches' shops. These were scores of shops built underneath the railway lines. The Japanese certainly used every available space and often I saw shops and offices built underneath buildings in underground arcades.

The 'underneath the arches' shops were also steel shuttered so I continued on to another shopping street called Motomachi. It was quite a lot further on and on the way I passed a number of Pachinko houses. They were already open and half full of customers. By the time I arrived at the Motomachi shops the shopkeepers were getting ready to open. The whole street was covered over by a domed roof and the space for pedestrians between shops was tiled. The tiles were glistening with water where the shopkeepers had recently washed them down. Again this was a sign of the Japanese people's desire for cleanliness, not only did they keep their shops spotless but even the pavements outside!

I wandered quite a way and bought some postcards. The range of goods on sale was just as at Yokohama and it was a real pleasure to window-shop, however, I decided not to stay too long as I wanted to have a quick look around in Sannimijo Shopping Street as well.

Sannimijo was also completely covered and although far smaller than Motomachi contained just as many different kinds of shops. I spent so long looking at the goods on sale, the fresh flowers; the souvenirs; the cakes and the household goods that I had to rush back to the ship to arrive before the end of shore leave.

The stevedores completed the cargo on time and as soon as we'd had lunch it was time to leave Japan for Taiwan. It was raining heavily as we left the harbour and the crew on deck wore bright yellow oilskins. The next morning, however, dawned bright and sunny. We were in sight of land all that day as we passed the southern Japanese islands of Shikoku and Kyushu and then the chain of volcanic islands that run down almost to Taiwan in the south and up to the Kuril islands in the north. We passed very close to one of the volcanos Io Shima, which was 323 feet high. Through binoculars I could see steam and smoke coming from its craters in puffs.

In the early evening while I was writing letters to go with Christmas cards, I noticed that I was beginning to get very hot, but there were no other signs of the weather we were about to experience. When I went up on the bridge at about 10 p.m., a wind was starting to blow and the tops of the waves were lifting off in white spray. By the end of the watch the ship was rolling violently. The waves and the swell were still only moderate at about ten to twelve feet high but the ship was virtually empty of cargo and gave us a very rough ride.

At 12.30 a.m. I awoke from a light sleep on hearing a bang and feeling a shake. At first, in my drowsy state, I thought the ship had hit something. I sat up in bed and was about to put on my lifejacket and rush outside when the ship took a roll the other way and I realised that the whole bunk was moving on its base and it had been that banging as it hit the bulkhead! It was a very strange sensation. I got up and secured everything that seemed loose although it was difficult to move about while the ship was rolling so violently. Colin came into the cabin whilst I was still precariously trying to silence all my belongings, he helped me, and then we went to bed but it was impossible to sleep.

Now and again we heard another crash somewhere in the distance, on deck or in one of the other cabins, but after a while we became so used to hearing them we hardly noticed. Colin tried to sleep on the daybed hoping that, as it was placed in the fore and aft of the ship, it would be easier to stay in one position. Unfortunately, however although he didn't fall off, he was kept awake because the rolls were nearly pulling the skin from his body! We tried every position and angle possible and tried to wedge ourselves in comfortable positions with our life jackets. It was hopeless, however, and after two hours when we were just about to give up, and had run out of names to call the ship, she settled down a little and at long last we were able to sleep a little between the more violent rolls.

When morning arrived we felt more tired than when we had gone to bed but we staggered from the bunk trying to get adjusted to walking without bumping into things. When I entered the day room I realised that I hadn't in fact secured everything the night before. The carpet looked like a cultivated garden, as it was covered with earth from the pot, which until that night, had contained a healthy green plant! There were a few other things mingled in the dirt, an ash tray, and all the rubbish from the waste paper basket. The whole mess took nearly an hour to clear up and just as I was finishing, we took another huge roll and the remainder of the earth and plant, which I thought I had put in a safe place, came crashing down again and showered me with dirt and leaves.

When I went up on the bridge the trail of destruction could be seen on every deck. Chairs lay at weird angles, the saloon tables were completely devoid of cutlery and condiments and the stewards rushed around with brooms and buckets of water trying to clear the debris.

The mess in our cabin had been minor compared with others. The Old Man's cabin was a complete wreck with chairs and tables in a crazy mass in the middle of the floor, topped by an upside down television. The fridge in the Sparky's cabin had come away from the wall and crashed into the bulkhead throwing the contents merrily around, and the fourth engineer found the top of a 'securely fixed' table on the other side of his cabin in two pieces!

The ship continued to roll throughout the day but by the afternoon we were so worn out we were able to sleep for a while and by evening calm was returning.

Chapter 11

KEELUNG AND THE FRESH FOOD MARKET

We arrived at Keelung, Taiwan, the next morning but were told that we must anchor until the next day as there was no berth ready immediately. I went out on deck to survey the distant shoreline which was surmounted by densely-wooded hills and mountains. The sea was a beautiful deep turquoise colour and I remembered that it had been the same when I visited Taiwan the year before. Then it had been midsummer with temperatures around 100 degrees Fahrenheit, but now it was winter and quite chilly.

We anchored all night and most of the following day but at about 3.00 p.m. a pilot boarded and we headed for the harbour entrance. It was well guarded with sea walls and cliffs and I noticed a number of port buildings with observation towers along the shore. They enabled the officials to make a close check of every vessel entering, so vital because of the constant threat from their arch enemies, China, just across the water.

We didn't go directly alongside but anchored in the inner harbour for a short while until the Customs and Immigration had carried out their various checks. There were five other ships also anchored alongside us and nearby bright purple lights flickered from welding torches at a shipbuilding yard. By the time the formalities were completed it was nearly dark although only 4.30 p.m. We made our way, aided by tugs, to our berth.

On one of the surrounding hillsides, I could see a huge white statue of a woman and several highly decorated pagoda-shaped buildings which were illuminated by strong floodlights. There were several Naval ships alongside the wharves and as we passed they were in the middle of lowering their flags for the night. As the flags fluttered towards the deck, a number of shrill whistles filled the air. Our Secuny went onto the poop deck to dip our National flag which was always done as a gesture of respect towards every Naval vessel that we passed.

We were berthed alongside the passenger terminal which was lined with lorries awaiting our cargo. Again it was decided that the stevedores should work all night to effect a quick turn around and although, at first, they seemed to be in a hurry to get started, they didn't actually begin discharging until around 6.00 p.m. Several of the Officers went up the road, but as Colin was working I decided that I would wait until daylight before venturing ashore.

By midnight, the cargo for discharge had been taken ashore and the stevedores started to load paper bags, badminton rackets, electrical goods, garments, baseballs, umbrellas, iron wire, electrical goods, and automobile parts for Mexico and Central America.

We were berthed so close to the town, that we could see the main streets from the porthole of our cabin. Traffic hurtled along the road that ran close by and the neon lights of shops and bars threw multi-coloured reflections into the harbour water.

The next morning dawned bright and, after tidying the cabin of Colin's usual trail of clothes, I prepared to go ashore after checking carefully that I had my pass. Outside it was humid and I was glad that I'd decided not to wear a coat. On the previous voyage I had visited Koa Hsuing in the south of Taiwan so I knew roughly what to expect. I was still looking forward to discovering Keelung Harbour. As I walked towards the town I looked at the passersby. Most of the inhabitants of the island are Chinese who flew the mainland when the Communists took over, however, there are still many native Taiwanese Indians. The people on the streets didn't seem anywhere near as clean as the Japanese but the women were fairly well dressed. The men, on the other hand, appeared very shoddy, and untidy and the children were positively dirty. The streets were reasonably clear of litter but very dirty. Spitting on the pavement was common practise and so they were obnoxious to walk on. I had also seen spitting in Japan but in most cases they used the gutter.

I also couldn't help noticing that the sewage system was not underground but merely channels about two feet deep covered by stone slabs. The slabs have slits cut into them to allow in waste water from the streets. In Kao Hsuing the smells from the sewers had been terrible and I often saw rats in and out of them, however, here in Keelung, because it was cooler, the smell wasn't so bad and I didn't see any rats.

A pedestrian bridge straddled the busy harbour road and I had to cross it to get to the main streets. From the top, I had a good view of my surroundings. The town was built in a bowl of hills with the harbour waters in the bottom and houses radiating up the sides. For some reason, the town looked unusual and then I suddenly realised why. The houses had been built among the trees and rocks which gave it a casual green appearance. There were houses built in every location and some were so high up the hillside they looked as if they would come tumbling down any minute. Most of the houses were small, square and built of concrete, and were very uninteresting and grey to look at, but, here and there, I could see older wooden ones which had high roofs covered in earthy-red tiles.

As I stood on the bridge looking around, people hustled past and traffic roared underneath. There was a continual line of traffic on the road, hundreds of cars, mainly Japanese-made, interspersed with noisy buses and hooting taxis. There were also scores of three-wheel vans. Most of them were motorised and looked like milk floats. I wanted a belt, so I went over to the shop, as one would in England, to have a look. There was a striped webbing belt lying on the counter, so I picked it up to get a closer look. Before I realised what was happening, the shopkeeper tried the belt around my waist; cut it down to size; wrapped it up; and stood there waiting for me to pay for it. I suddenly realised my mistake. I had had no intention of buying the belt. I had merely been looking at it and had only U.S. dollars anyway so I couldn't pay him. I simply had to walk away leaving the wrapped belt on the counter. When the shopkeeper got over his initial shock, and realised what I was doing, he started shouting at me in Taiwanese. I could only guess what he was saying. After that embarrassing escapade, I never again touched anything unless I had decided to buy it!

After my hasty retreat, and when I had at least two streets between myself and the angry shopkeeper, I slowed down, and on turning a corner came across an open air market. At the edges of the market the locals had set up stalls and wheelbarrows displaying shoes and clothes but most of the stalls were selling food. The streets were so narrow because the stalls were set up right in front of the shops. They were so closely packed that they blocked the light from the shops.

The variety of food on sale was incredible but the state of hygiene and the treatment of numerous live animals was terrible. One stall was selling fish. Most of it was dead and lay on dirty trays waiting to be selected, weighed and stuffed into plastic bags. Some of the fish, however, was still alive swimming feebly around in bowls of aerated water. When a customer selected one it was immediately taken from the bow; decapitated and bundled bloody and trailing entrails into a plastic bag. Several bowls containing the fish had pieces of entrails floating around in them amongst the poor fish that remained. I didn't recognise many of the fish as there were so many on display but I did see prawns, eels, small sharks, mackerel, squid and crabs. The crabs were also alive but not in water. Instead they were tied together with pieces of string. Their eyes bulged out on stalks as they tried desperately to get away. Their efforts, however, only resulted in the strings getting tighter and tighter.

There were also stalls selling meat and every type of offal imaginable, still oozing blood and collecting dust as it lay in the open. Then, after passing a number of fruit stalls which were grouped together, I arrived at the poultry stall and wished that I hadn't. The hens and ducks were still alive caged in baskets like lobsterpots. Customers queued up at the stall and selected the bird they required. The unfortunate bird was then dragged from its basket squawking, its neck wrung, its feathers ripped out and its entrails removed, all in a matter of minutes. Before handing over the still warm bird, the stall holder washed it in a bucket of bloody water and put it in a polythene bag. The stall also served up cooked birds and I noticed someone sitting next to the caged birds eating a chicken leg! The remaining birds were terrified. They knew what was happening to their former colleagues and seemed to be staring agog at the man who was by now picking at the bone.

I suddenly became aware of an awful smell that was emanating from the stall, a mixture of blood, excreta, frying chicken, fear and death and when I looked down I noticed that I was standing in a pool of blood and entrails. It was all too much for me and I beat a hasty retreat, my stomach heaving and face green. I didn't stop until I was several streets away. It had been a horrible experience and to me it seemed incredible that people could be so inhumane and unhygienic.

The whole episode left me feeling a bit queasy but I continued window-shopping until I came to the edge of town where the houses and shops thinned out dramatically and there were no more streets, just a few houses dotted amongst the trees. I decided that was far enough for me to venture and returned to the ship.

I made sure that I kept well away from the market on the way back but I had to pass a street of refreshment stalls. Each stall had its own table and chairs which were set up alongside it and a large cauldron of black cooking oil bubbling over a fire inside the stall. I wasn't feeling at all hungry after my experience in the market but when I saw the things that were being cooked in the cauldrons I lost my appetite even more! There was a selection of meat, fish, frogs, snake, and offal, even ears, feet and eyes! These were served with bowls of slimy noodles or rice swimming in bowls of brown runny gravy. The locals seemed to like eating outside and although it was only 11 a.m. the grimy tables were surrounded with people eating hungrily. As soon as one customer finished his bowl was collected dipped in a bucket of dirty water that looked like it had been there several days, and then used for the next customer!

When I got back to the ship it was lunchtime but I couldn't even force myself to eat! Colin had worked the morning cargo watch and so after lunch he decided to snatch an hour from his sleep to have a look ashore. I went with him and then, when he returned to the ship I hailed a taxi to take me to the buildings at the top of the hill. Earlier I had asked one of the shop assistants about the buildings and she had explained that they were part of a park called Chung Cheung Park. She had kindly given me a slip of paper with the name of the park written in Chinese, so, although the taxi driver couldn't speak English I was able to communicate the destination to him.

At first we travelled through narrow streets and then wound up the hillside on a tarmac road which had several hairpin bends in it. It took about ten minutes to get to the top so I was amazed when the fare was only 16NT approximately 12p!

Most of the buildings in the park and the statue of a woman, were perched on a plateau at the top of the hill, above the taxi's dropping off point but the pagodas were on the side of the hill down a slightly sloping gravel path. I decided to visit the pagodas first. As I got closer, I could see that what at first looked like three pagodas, was in fact one building in three sections. The central pagoda section was one floor higher than the other two but they were joined by a diagonal flight of steps that led from the top floor of the smaller pagodas to the fourth and highest floor of the central one. The building looked modern and was painted brightly, however, the design and the wall carvings were obviously of traditional design. Each pagoda section of the building was similar in construction, round and open-sided, although the bottom two floors had been walled in at a later stage and seemed to be used for accommodation. The other floors simply had waist high balustrades running around them. Each floor was held up by six decorative columns and on top of each section was a many sectioned roof, covered with orange tiles that sparkled in the sunlight.

There were large double doors at the front of the central pagoda and open archways leading into the ones at each side. The doors, however, were locked so I went into one of the side pagoda sections and up some stairs to the first floor. Unfortunately that was as far as I could get as doors at the top of the stairs were also locked. There was, however, a walkway under the pagoda which I reached by going down a flight of narrow steps. From the walkway there was a good view of the harbour and town. I could see the Amparo lying alongside the passenger terminal and behind her the spread of houses and trees that made up Keelung. It was like looking at a picture postcard: sampling the oriental atmosphere without being able to smell the oriental smells!

After a while I climbed to the other buildings on the plateau. The road was very steep and several buses laboured past me on their way to the top. The road, at one point, was being repaired. Men were actually doing the repair work but women were carrying the gravel and sand that was being used for the repair. They carried the materials in open-ended wicker-work baskets which were attached to yokes. The women toiled up and down the road with baskets full of heavy materials and it became quite obvious that there was no women's liberation movement in Taiwan. The women did all the menial tasks whilst the men were definitely the bosses. Seeing the women carriers here reminded me of the women dock workers in Koa Hsiung. The ship I had been on then was discharging grain into hoppers and then into sacks. It was the women's job to sew up the sacks and they worked from twelve to eighteen hours in the blistering heat. I had also noticed that morning that the rubbish collectors and street sweepers were women.

When I got to the top of the road I stopped to have a look around. Now I could see the view on the opposite side to the harbour. Besides houses, there were a number of schools built amongst the trees on the hillsides. Each school was in an elevated position and surrounded by large playgrounds. The schools looked fairly modern and were several stories high and built of concrete. Most of the pupils seemed to be outside in the playgrounds and they all wore identical military-style uniforms.

The buildings which I had come to see were on the highest part of the hill, and after leaving the road, I had to continue up a footpath to get to them. I passed a large white statue of a Buddha which I hadn't been able to see from below. He had several smaller what looked like Buddhas in light blue coats climbing all over him. Eventually I reached the base of the huge white statue of a woman. She towered some thirty feet above me. The watchkeeper had told me that she was the goddess of the sea and was positioned on the hill top to oversee the boats and ships below. Her robes shone white in the bright afternoon sunlight. Looking up I could see that she had a very stern look on her face and she looked very matronly. In her perfectly sculptured hands she held a scroll.

Behind the statue were the buildings. One of them was a souvenir shop, the other was called Shihtung Puchi temple. It was another modern building, square and solid, but quite decorative with a row of vermillion-painted columns along the front and a shining orange roof like the ones on the pagoda. I couldn't get inside as all the doors were tightly locked so instead, I walked back to the edge of the hill to take a photograph of the statue.

There were two Chinese men there flying kites in the breeze. The kites were ingeniously designed. They were shaped like birds and flapped their wings in exactly the same way as real life birds. When I realised that they were selling the kites I couldn't resist buying one as a present.

I didn't have to go back down the road to the town as there was a footpath and steps down the hillside through the park. The path wound between shrubs, playgrounds and decorated shelters. Halfway down, there was another temple building which had a pond and a fountain outside it. I had a look around the building but again found that it was locked. The last flight of steps, which led to street level, was almost vertical and I had to cling to the handrail in the centre to stop myself from falling. When I got to the bottom I realised that I was only a couple of streets away from the ship, so after another quick look around the souvenir shops, I made my way back.

While I was drinking coffee at afternoon Smoko, I suddenly heard noises like rifle shots outside the cabin. I jumped up quite startled and looked out of the porthole to see two small working boats circling the harbour. One was towing the other and on the deck of the second one there was a man holding a long pole which had fire crackers attached to it on a string. As the string burnt the fire crackers ignited and one by one they exploded like reports from a gun. When the boats had made three circuits of the harbour, dozens more fire cracker strings were set off on the group of boats alongside a nearby jetty. The noise was ear splitting, even from inside, it sounded like a pitch battle was taking place. The fire crackers banged away for another ten minutes, until at last, peace reigned again over the harbour. Later the agent told us that the boat being towed was brand new and the ceremony had been to celebrate its launching. The fire crackers were supposed to ward off any evil spirits that had got on the boat while it was being built. He told us that the fishermen were extremely superstitious, like all seamen, and that their crews always dropped prayer papers over the side of the boat as they left harbour, to ensure a good catch.

We sailed at 9.00 p.m. that evening. At first, the pilot had difficulty turning the ship around in the narrow harbour, but, eventually, with the aid of a tug, we were facing the right direction and steaming towards the distant breakwater. Looking back towards the town I could see the neon lights flashing and the sea goddess and pagoda shining in the floodlights.

CHAPTER 12

HONG KONG AND THE RICKSHAW MAN

When I woke the next morning there was a full-scale gale blowing and at 8.00 a.m. a Monsoon wind of force 9 on the Beaufort scale (over 40 knots) was recorded in the log book. The swell and wind waves were the highest we'd seen during the trip. The Amparo sailed on as steady as a rock without a single roll, pitch or corkscrew. I couldn't believe it and wondered at first whether I was awake but Colin explained that as the massive waves were following us they simply pushed us along without disturbing the ship at all. There was, however, a danger of 'pooping' – the waves rising above the stern and landing on the poopdeck, which might swamp the after end and possibly cause some damage, so, to minimise the danger the engine revolutions were reduced.

I saw several ships coming in the opposite direction. They were fighting against the weather and they were having a rough ride and I hoped that when we returned the weather would be better.

At 5.30 a.m. the next morning the Mate asked Colin to say that the Hong Kong pilot was expected aboard at any minute. I was determined not to miss anything so I dressed hurriedly and went on the promenade deck. It was still very dark, with no sign of sunrise but the Pilot didn't arrive until 6 a.m. and by then it was getting light. As we made our way towards the Quarantine anchorage, I noticed that there were a lot of ships at anchor around us, including two passenger ships. The Quarantine anchorage turned out to be only half a mile from our previous position and soon we were stopped again waiting for the officials to arrive. The sun edged its way over the surrounding hillsides but it was very misty and I still couldn't see our surroundings well.

We had to wait until 9.30 a.m. for the Customs and Immigration officials to arrive and so I wished I hadn't got up so early. At last, however, we made our way towards Victoria harbour. I had read in the pilot book that Hong Kong consisted of the island called Hong Kong as well as the piece of the mainland that stretched from Kowloon, on the other side of the harbour, to the Chinese border, twenty miles inland. There were only a few quays which were used for naval vessels and passenger boats, so merchant ships anchored in Victoria harbour between the island and the mainland, discharging and loading from barges.

As we made our way towards the allotted anchorage pontoon, I began to feel the romantic atmosphere which I had always associated with Hong Kong. The waters in the harbour were greeny-turquoise colour and were constantly awash with the bow-waves of every type of water craft imaginable. There were passenger ferries, hydrofoils, hovercraft, fishing boats, Chinese junks, liberty boats, pilot boats, barges, bunker barges, store-carrying boats, mail boats, car ferries, as well as container ships; gas carriers; general cargo ships; bulk cargo ships; and passenger ships. On both sides of the harbour, were rolling wooded hills which surrounded the two main towns of the colony. Victoria, the business and commercial centre on the island, and Kowloon on the mainland. The towns were a mass of skyscrapers with sheer walls of concrete and thousands of symmetrical windows. They looked as if they were competing for superiority, like trees in a rainforest! The whole scene was shrouded in haze and warmed by the rising sun.

As soon as we dropped anchor, boats converged upon us and within minutes we were surrounded by liberty boats, a pilot boat and several barges. A flat-decked boat which had portable steps on it was tied up alongside our gangway to act as a jetty and soon the passengers from the boats were jumping from it and onto the swaying gangway. The ship's agent and his followers boarded and I noticed, with pleasure, that one was carrying a mailbag. The pilot then left the ship and the pilot boat joined the throng and chugged off in the direction of Kowloon. This left room for the liberty boats to pull alongside and drop the gangs of stevedores who swarmed aboard carrying their lunch in shopping bags.

As I looked around, I noticed that the barges which contained our cargo had already tied up alongside. They were all similar in design with varnished hulls, rounded at the bow and flat at the stern, and a large forward hold which could be covered by a tarpaulin spread on poles.

The superstructure of the barges, however, gave them each an individual appearance because they were covered in carvings and gaily painted in different styles.

The closest barge was tied alongside the gangway and by looking over the side I could see the people on deck. I suddenly realised that not only were they barges but houseboats too! The owners' whole family lived on board. I saw mothers, children and dogs and there was even washing hanging out to dry on the deckheads and baskets of chicken and pot plants on the main deck.

When the barge was underway each member of the family had a job. The father did the steering and navigating, the mother was in charge of the ropes, and tying up, and the children ran along the deck hanging wicker baskets over the side to act as fenders when the barge came alongside. As soon as they were securely tied up, however, the women went back to their washing and cooking and cleaning and the children resumed their play, it seemed a perfect sort of life.

As I was watching the activity on board, the barges and a 'bum' boat arrived. I had seen similar ones before in Singapore harbour and knew that they carried hawkers and their wares from the shore to ships at anchor. Competition amongst them was great and the first one to arrive claimed the best 'selling' position. It tied up at the stern and somehow its occupants got on board and started to winch their wares up after them. They moved quickly unpacking boxes and drawers and it wasn't long before all their goods were displayed on the Promenade deck. They sold everything a seaman could possibly want from shaving cream and postcards to radios and underwear. Another vendor had arrived on board by this time and he set up shop in the alleyway next to the bar. He was selling Happy Coats (short silk dressing gowns embroidered with dragons and flowers) and a selection of decorated cushion covers.

After reading the mail which we had received, I went out onto the Promenade deck. The sun was now high in the sky and really warm and the disturbed water around the ship sparkled in its light. There was so much going on in the harbour that I spent the rest of the morning just watching.

Now that we had reached Hong Kong our passengers were leaving us. Over the previous four weeks we had become friends and it was a sad moment when a Liberty boat arrived to take them ashore. We all shook hands and they laboured down the gangway with their luggage, to start the next stage of their journeys: the Mexican to India; and the Swiss boys on round the world. We waved until they merged into the hustle and bustle of other little boats.

Just before lunch a notice was posted outside the bar listing the times of the Liberty boats that had been hired to take people ashore. The first was scheduled for 1.30 p.m.. I knew that Colin wouldn't be able to get ashore because cargo was being worked around the clock but I was determined to go as soon as possible. The Engineers had the afternoon off and several of the lads had decided to go ashore too. We all laughed when they said they were going shopping and sightseeing as we knew they would end up in one of the bars as usual.

At 1.30 p.m. precisely the liberty boat arrived and we clambered aboard armed with cameras and Hong Kong dollars. The boat was really low in the water and as we chugged off I felt even more excited to be part of the hustle and bustle of the harbour. Looking back I could see our 'home' with all her barges and boats in attendance but soon she was lost amongst the other ships.

The agent had told us that the island would be pretty dead as on Saturday most of the shops were closed. He advised instead to go to Kowloon where everything would be open and the liberty boat owner agreed to take us directly there although his landing stage was on the island. As we got close we crossed in front of several passenger and car ferries that plied between Kowloon and the island and it wasn't long before we were tying up next to the passenger terminal. We scrambled ashore and made our way towards the centre past the bus station and the huge towering Hong Kong hotel. I was almost immediately disappointed by the lack of atmosphere. I had always imagined Hong Kong as a romantic oriental spectacle and the harbour had contained all my imaginations, but, now that I was ashore amongst towering concrete buildings and wide impersonal streets, the imagined atmosphere dissolved.

As I walked down Canton Street, I found it strange to hear people speaking English and to see the women with their typical English Rose complexions. I knew that I wouldn't get lost ashore here, and it really reassured me. The red double-decker buses that milled around amongst the traffic added to the familiar scene and if it hadn't been for the number of Chinese people thronging the pavements, I could have imagined myself in London.

On the way to the centre I passed a collection of food stalls, which had bubbling cauldrons of black cooking oil alongside them, just like the ones I had seen in Taiwan. For a moment the oriental atmosphere returned but as soon as I reached the shops it faded again. I had no map or directions and consequently ended up in the tourist area of town. Of course I was a tourist but one who prefers to see other things then souvenir shops. Every shop was aimed at the tourist and sold either jewellery; cameras; electrical goods; clothes and souvenirs. Above and below the shops were sauna rooms; bars; and saloons. There were several shopping arcades, which were modern and concrete but they didn't sell everyday items, only tourist things. I wanted to buy some writing paper but none of the shops sold such a normal thing as that and I had to search for ages before I discovered a department store that did. The store could easily have been a Debenhams and even accepted sterling. As I wandered around amongst the shops I realised that if I looked hard enough the Orient was there hidden behind concrete facades.

I saw wizened Chinese men peeping through the bars of money changing cubicles, which promised to change any currency into any currency. There were live fish in a tank outside a restaurant waiting to be selected from the menu, and a small shop selling a vast array of herbs and spices. I even saw signs saying 'No Spitting'. On the surface, however, the centre of Kowloon wasn't Chinese, it was British. I wondered if I had several days to spare whether I could discover, in the suburbs, and countryside, the oriental sights and atmosphere that I had imagined or whether the English influence had changed it all.

I finally succumbed to the draw of the souvenir shops and became a typical tourist. I went in and out of the shops looking at jade statues, ivory necklaces and embroidered silk pictures, but I was especially interested in the Mah Jong games. I have often played Mah Jong in England with a set that Colin's father had brought in Hong Kong, twenty years before. His set is a real work of art and his tiles are made from bamboo and ivory. I wondered if it was still possible to get such a set and was hoping not to find still being used. Sad to say I managed eventually to run one to ground. Prices had rocketed in the intervening years and each tile only had a sliver of ivory on it. The lowest price the shopkeeper would accept was £40. I thoroughly did not agree with ivory being used so I brought a plastic and bamboo set for £6!

I had decided to catch the 5.00 p.m. liberty boat back to the ship so all too soon I had to make my way back to the 'Star' ferry terminal to catch a ferry to the island. As I passed through the turnstile at the terminal an attendant took my 30cents (about 6p) fare and I walked along a covered jetty to the waiting ferry. As soon as we were out in the harbour again the romantic atmosphere came flooding back until a few minutes later we arrived at the other side and I made my way back amongst the shadows of the towering buildings of Victoria.

I asked several people the way to Blake Pier where I was to catch the liberty boat back to the ship. It had only just gone 4 p.m. so I thought that I would locate the pier first before having a quick look about Victoria. Nobody, however, seemed to know where it was but a little Chinese man dressed in worn clothes came up to me mumbling something and pointing to a bright red rickshaw that was standing near the pavement, he seemed most insistent that he take me to Blake Pier in the rickshaw so, as could think of no other way of finding it, I repeated Blake Pier and clambered in. The little man stood between the shafts and off we went along the waterfront.

It turned out to be a most embarrassing ride as everyone looked up from what they were doing to stare at me, almost as if I was committing some sort of crime by riding in a rickshaw. At least ten minutes later the little man came to a halt and I was very glad to get out. I went to give him some coins but he said 'paper, paper.' I pulled out my two remaining 10 Hong Kong dollar notes and he took them both before I worked out that he had charged me over £2. By that, he was jogging off in the opposite direction so that there was nothing I could do.

I made my way down to the nearby pier and asked man to confirm that I was at Blake Pier as there were no signs. I was horrified when he explained that Blake Pier was back next to the Star Ferry terminal Where the rickshaw man had picked me up!

I was livid. By this time it was 4.30 p.m. but the man said that if I walked quickly I would get back in time for the liberty boat. I rushed back down the road, past all the people who had stared at me before. They stared even harder this time and I could feel my face reddening with fury and embarrassment.

I arrived back outside the ferry terminal hot, sweaty and very angry. To my amazement the rickshaw man had returned and he sat by his rickshaw chatting to some colleagues. I wondered whether I had made it clear enough what that I wanted Blake Pier when he picked me up but I was sure that I had and by now I was so cross that I stormed up to him and demanded to know why he had taken me to the wrong place. He made out he didn't understand me which made me even more angry. He even started to walk off but I was determined not to be outdone and stood in front of him with my hand out asking him for my money back. He must have understood that because he reached into his pocket and produced one of the 10 dollar notes. By this time passersby had stopped and were looking with interest, so I pocketed the note and walked off the Blake Pier, a stone's throw away.

When I got there several of the officers from the Amparo were waiting and, after I had related my adventures with the rickshaw man, I felt much better and soon we were talking about our purchases and impressions of Hong Kong. It wasn't long before the liberty boat arrived and we made our way back to the ship. By the time we reached her my anger had almost completely disappeared along with the sun that was sinking below the distant hills.

During the evening I discussed my disappointments about Hong Kong with the others and most of them agreed with me, however, one of the engineers who had crossed over to Victoria early in the afternoon said that he had found a street where people were sitting outside carving wood and weaving cloth and that there had been cobblers shops, Chinese houses and parks.

It took until 3 a.m. the following morning to complete cargo. When I asked Colin what we had loaded he said 'You name it......... we loaded it!' and someone behind him said 'Yes and ....all made in Hong Kong!'

CHAPTER 13

KOBE REVISITED AND ROKKO MOUNTAIN

At 7 a.m. the next morning, Sunday 4th December, we set sail for Japan again. The haze which had been there the previous morning, again shrouded the colony and it wasn't until the sun was fairly high, that I could see anything of the island as we passed it. By 9.00 a.m., however, it was clear enough to take some photographs. We passed little fishing junks, wooded hills, high mountains, and skyscraper buildings. There were also tiny bays surrounded by high cliffs and I couldn't help wishing that I'd had time to discover a bit more of Hong Kong.

That afternoon, as we steamed up the Chinese coast, I looked out of the porthole and saw that we were passing Chinese junks. When I went out on to deck to get a better view, I realised that there were hundreds of them, all around. Most of them had their sails rigged. They were ribbed sails and looked like huge fans. The junks were a splendid sight as they sailed along in the strong wind or lay wallowing with their nets trailing along behind them. We passed very close to one and I could see the men on deck hauling in the nets. We sailed between and around the junks for nearly two hours but eventually the last of them disappeared over the horizon.

On the first day of our return trip to Japan, we received warnings of a circular storm called Typhoon Lucy. Lucy had formed just east of the Philippine Islands and when she had filled, started to move at eight knots northwards towards our position in the South China Sea. Her movements were watched carefully so that avoiding action could be taken if necessary, but on the third day the weather report showed that she was racing at eighteen knots north eastward into the Pacific Ocean where she eventually died out.

Also during the passage we received news of the third engineer. He was recovering slowly and wouldn't be rejoining the ship until the last day before our departure from Japan. His toe was obviously causing more trouble that at first envisaged.

We arrived off Kobe at 10 p.m. on 7th December and anchored overnight in the eastern anchorage. At 7 a.m. the next morning, however, we went alongside Maya Pier. There wasn't much cargo to load at Kobe so we knew that we wouldn't be there long and in the end it was decided that we would be sailing again that evening. I had decided to visit Mt. Rokko, the highest peak of the mountain range behind Kobe. I left the ship as soon as I could.

Maya pier was nearly two miles from Kobe town centre, but a city bus ran along the road to the end of the pier. I could see from the map that I had acquired from the Missions to Seaman, how many stops I had to pass before getting off so I decided to catch a bus. I had only to wait a few minutes before a green single deck bus arrived. I tried to get in the front door like the buses in England, but I suddenly realised that the double doors at the centre of the bus were for boarding, so, feeling rather stupid, I had to walk back down the pavement and get on through the right doors! I only just avoided making another mistake after that. I thought I had to pay the fare straight away but the driver didn't wait for that, he pulled off straight away instead, and as there was no conductor I just sat down and started to count the stops. It was then that I realised that fares were paid on leaving the bus and that as the fare was 45yen for one stop and then 90yen for more than one, the money was simply dropped into a collecting machine by the driver.

I soon began to recognise my surroundings and when we reached Flower Road I walked up to the box and dropped my 90 yen into it and got off, as if I had been travelling on Japanese buses all my life!

I had two letters to post for the Captain and some shopping to get. I decided to do that first before attempting to find my way to the mountains. After leaving the Post Office I found the Motomachi Shopping Centre. Being on the ship and cut off from the rest of the world I had forgotten how close we were to Christmas but I was soon reminded of it by the decorations in the Arcade and the piped Christmas Carols that filled the air. I was a bit surprised by the festive surroundings. I thought that the majority of Japanese, being Buddhists, didn't celebrate Christmas. It was lovely to hear the carols, however, and it really put me in a festive mood. I bought some Christmas cards and wandered among the shops noticing special stalls that had been set up outside department stores. They were selling special Christmas promotions which included Christmas cakes and biscuits and festively decorated accompaniments for the kimono: bands, ties, frills, combs, handkerchiefs, bags and purses. There was also a stall outside one of the toy shops that sold brown teddy bears which played 'Rudolf the red nosed reindeer' on drums!

It was nearly midday by the time I dragged myself away from the shops and made my way to the stations. This time I knew where to go because we had changed at Rokko station when going to Kyoto. I even knew how many stations we had to pass through so I boarded that train on platform two with quiet confidence and settled down for the journey. After nearly quarter of an hour however, we hadn't stopped at a single station and I began to get a bit concerned. I searched for someone to consult but it was quite a while before I could find anyone that could speak English and I was beginning to panic. In the end, however, a very nice Japanese lady came to my rescue and explained that I had got on a through train, instead of the one that stopped at all the little stations! I felt very helpless as we sped further and further away but the lady explained that soon we would stop and I could get out, change platforms, and return to Rokko on another train. We seemed to go on and on but, eventually, with a hiss of air brakes we pulled up at Nishinomiya station and, thanking the lady profusely, I thankfully got out.

I had to ask several people before I found the right platform for my return to Rokko and, when the train pulled up, I was very careful to ask if it stopped at all the stations. Eventually, however, I arrived on Rokko station platform in one piece although feeling rather flustered and stupid! I decided that, as I wasn't as good as I thought I was travelling on public transport I wouldn't try to find the city bus but would take a taxi to the Rokko cable car station. I soon found one and explained where I wanted to go to the driver. He seemed a little surprised that I didn't want to go all the way to the top of the mountain in the taxi but, as it was, the trip to the cable car station cost 510yen, a fortune compared with 90yen for the journey from Kobe.

The cable station was very smart, painted white with a thatched roof which reminded me of stations in Switzerland. A cable car stood waiting inside. It was due to leave so I paid my fare and hurriedly made my way up the steep steps to board it. As I got on I noticed that it was about the size of a single railway carriage but was shaped so that it fitted diagonally against the mountain at an angle of about 60 degrees. The seats were placed down its length in steps, so that the passengers sat horizontally looking at the driver below. The car ran on wires, it also had guide wheels placed at regular intervals to hold it on course. There was a whirr from the wires as we moved and as the car passed over the wheels it banged rather violently. We rose very steeply and soon the station was many feet below us. The sides of the car were open and I could see that the mountainside was completely covered with trees and undergrowth. Many of the trees were evergreen but they were interspersed with clumps of deciduous trees resplendent in their autumn colours. The smell of the trees drifted into the car and, as we got higher, the air became thinner. We climbed and climbed, higher and higher, and my ears popped several times. Soft music was played to us during the journey and every now and again a woman's voice interrupted with a Japanese narrative on our surroundings. Half way up the mountainside the line split into two. Another car appeared as we approached the division and banged its way downwards leaving the guide wheels spinning madly. Almost immediately the line returned to a single track and I was glad that the drivers were practised at getting the cars to the passing place at the correct time. Higher and higher we rose and just as it seemed that we would climb forever, the car slowed down and we were at the summit station, 932 metres above sea level. The journey had taken 15 minutes.

As soon as I left the car I breathed in the pure mountain air. It was cool and refreshing and yet so thin that it was difficult to breathe if I walked quickly. Outside the station there was a huge map on a billboard but all the writing was only in Japanese so I couldn't understand it. I gathered, however, that to see everything I would have needed a car and supposed that was the reason the taxi driver had been so shocked, when I asked for the cable car. I could at least tell from the map that there was a skating pond; golf courses; lakes; scenic routes and ski slopes covering the mountain top.

I walked to the edge near the station to have a look at the view first but it was completely obliterated by a fine haze, although the sun shone brilliantly above. It had been quite cold on the ship but here on the mountain it was just refreshingly cool and there was no sign of the snow that we had seen on our earlier visit. From the station the road led in two directions. At first I walked to the left through thick green fir trees but the road seemed to lead downwards so I turned round and went the other way instead. As soon as the few passengers from the cable car were out of earshot, the silence was complete except for the twittering of birds in the tree tops. After the noise of the ship it seemed so quiet it was eerie.

Even at such a height, trees covered the mountainside. Besides the evergreens there were a number of deciduous varieties. I couldn't identify them but several were covered in berries: red; yellow; and bright purple in colour. As I walked along the road my peace was shattered every now and then by a car winding its way around hair pin bends. I hadn't realised that there were any people living on the mountain, so I was quite surprised, when I turned a corner and saw many, in fact probably more than a hundred, houses perched in little niches on the side of the mountain. It seemed that a lot of people, obviously the richer ones judging by the size and design of the houses, lived on the mountain and commuted to the town using the eight kilometre long road down the mountainside. On a far ridge, behind the houses, I could see a modern hotel and what had been described on the map as an observatory. A ropeway stretched from the cable car summit station, past the hotel, and on to the hot springs at Arima Spa which was in a gorge on the other side of the mountain. I had been told that the ropeway was closed during the winter but, as I walked on along the road, I saw a cable car swing out from the station and sway across on the ropeway above the sheer mountainside. After a while, I came to a junction where I left the road and took a pathway to the highest peak. The path rose gradually at first, but soon it became very steep. The trees on either side of the path were so thick that it was quite dark. Every now and then a little blue bird with a long black tail flew up from the path into nearby trees. After ten minutes steep climb, I eventually reached the summit. There were no trees on the very top but still plenty of grass and stretched out before me was a lush golf course.

I didn't have time to go any further so I retraced my steps to the station. It was almost as exhausting going down the path as it had been going up and my legs ached by the time I regained the road. As I was nearing the station, the cloud of haze suddenly lifted to reveal a wonderful panoramic view of Osaka bay and Kobe town. It was still too hazy to take photographs but I was able to make out the silhouette of the M.V. Amparo, as she lay alongside Mayo pier. The tourist map said that visitors to Rokko mountain should stay until nightfall when the view turned into a magnificent twinkling display but, of course, I couldn't stay that long unless I wanted to miss the ship! I had already stayed longer that I should have done.

When I arrived back at the lower cable car station, a bus was waiting. I asked a man who was walking down the steps, if the bus went to Rokko station. He said 'yes it does, and I'm the driver!' in perfect English. From then on my return journey went without a hitch. I got off at the right stop; I caught a train that stopped at Sannomiya station and even used the correct doors to get on the bus back to Mayo pier.

When I got back to the ship, I found a salesman for Satsuma china was on board. He had displays of his wares set up on a table in the bar. I had heard of Satsuma china before and I knew it was very high quality, egg-shell thin china, which was hand painted with traditional designs and pictures. The china on display was very beautiful. There were coffee and tea sets; vases and sake sets and ornaments. I could see right through the tea and coffee cups they were so thin and delicate. When Colin said I could have a coffee set for a Christmas present I jumped at the chance. Between us we selected a set with a black background decorated with gold pagodas and trees called Damascene design. As part of the service the salesman promised to send the set home for us by post and that if any of the pieces were damaged he would send replacements. A few weeks later we heard from Colin's parents that the set had arrived home safely beautifully packed in a small cardboard box.

At 9.00 p.m. that evening we left Kobe again and set sail for our next port, Nagoya.

CHAPTER 14

NAGOYA, YOKOHAMA AND SANKEI-EN GARDENS

By daybreak the following morning we were sailing through Ise bay to the harbour approaches of Nagoya. I read in the tourist pamphlet that Ise bay was famous for its cultured pearl farms, especially around Tobe in the south but, although I strained my eyes to catch a glimpse of them, I couldn't see anything except a deserted shoreline.

It had been hazy on our last visit to Nagoya, but this time it was clear and I could see our surroundings. There were hundreds of factories with smoking chimneys and quays covered with piles of sand and coal.

By the time we had tied up it was 2 p..m.. I consulted the chart to discover that we were even further from Nagoya than on our first visit. It had turned cold and threatened snow and rain, and, although there was no cargo being worked, Colin did the night on board duties so I decided to stay on board. We had a sociable evening in the bar that evening, playing darts and sampling the new brand of beer, San Miguel, which had recently arrived on board, and then we turned in to get a straight eight hours sleep.

In the morning I could see that we were berthed alongside a container quay and I watched the bustling activity with interest. I knew that containers were a relatively new idea but also that it was becoming more and more popular to ship cargo in containers. The theory behind the system is a good one, not only does it make stowage of small items easier, it discourages pilfering and speeds up the loading process.

There were hundreds of machines on the quay especially designed to deal with the containers and the management of the container terminal was excellent. Consequently containers were quickly loaded and discharged, stacked, stored or redirected with the minimum of handling. I was quite impressed by it all and watched for a long time, especially by the ease with which huge containers were lifted by large forklift trucks or specially adapted cranes onto long bases and within minutes were on their way to their destination.

Our cargo, resin, wasn't in containers but it was still loaded quickly and efficiently and by 9.00 p.m. we were ready to sail.

The passage to our next port, Yokohama, was uneventful and when we arrived it was just as sunny and warm as it had been two weeks earlier. After anchoring, for a short while we were taken alongside, this time, however, we only went as far as the first breakwater and were guided to No. 4 berth on Yamashita Pier. This meant that it was a bit further to walk to town but not excessively so.

As it was Sunday there were no stevedores waiting to rush aboard and start work so everyone was able to relax a little and after lunch Colin decided to come ashore to stretch his legs. The sun, although wintry, was warm and we strolled along happily towards the town. We were soon in China Town where the streets were thronged with people and their families. From there, we made our way to the Isetachi-Cho Shopping Centre where Christmas shopping was in full swing. Colin decided to buy himself a Christmas present and after visiting several watch shops he ended up with a Seiko Digital watch for less than half it would have cost him in England. He then decided that he had had enough shopping and wanted to take full advantage of his day off by relaxing aboard the ship. So we hailed a taxi. As we were getting in, however, we saw a very strange sight. Walking towards the shopping street were several young men dressed in black kimonos and traditional *geta* shoes. They looked to me like priests and they carried wooden flutes. Some of them were wearing the strangest hats I have ever seen. The hats were woven like baskets and were oval in shape with the bottoms cut off! They covered the whole head and rested on their shoulders. The men looked very peculiar walking along with these 'basket' hats on their heads and for a while I couldn't make out why they didn't fall over obstacles in the street but then I noticed that each basket was equipped with slits for breathing and seeing through. When the Chief Steward's wife visited the ship several days later, I asked her if she knew what, or rather who, they were. She said she wasn't sure but thought that they were novice monks. She explained that it was very unusual to see them in the streets but that they may be practising for one of the New Year Festivals.

The next day I went ashore to visit Sankei-en gardens. The weather had changed completely from the previous day and it was cold, windy and threatening rain. However, we didn't know how long we would be in port and I was determined to see as much as possible whilst we were there. I caught a bus outside the gates and was surprised to see people getting on through the front doors and paying on entry as well as getting on the side doors and paying on exit. I began to wonder if in fact I hadn't made such a big mistake in Kobe after all! I nearly missed the stop I wanted to get off at but thanks, once again, to a kind Japanese lady, I just realised in time. The Sankei-en gardens were situated two blocks away from the bus stop and the area that I walked through was a very high-class suburb. All the houses were grand and modern and each had a big car in the garage. Although the houses were modern their design was traditional with many roofs and balconies and wooden shutters and although some had concrete walls the majority were constructed totally of wood. They all had high walls around their gardens but several had the gates open so that you could see inside. In some of the gardens I noticed orange trees that still had fruit on them. I couldn't resist photographing them. The locals must have thought me very strange. When I got back to the ship the Mate told me that oranges growing on trees had fascinated his wife also and that once, whilst she was looking at them, the occupant of the house came out and picked some for her!

Sankei-en gardens were also walled and outside there were ticket machines like at railway stations. I purchased a ticket for 100 yen and went inside. The scene that lay before me would have delighted any photographer and could have easily adorned a high class calendar. Nearest to me there was a large still lake surrounded by trees, bushes and well-kept lawns and on the hill behind the lake the top story of a pagoda peeped out above fir trees. On the lake there were numerous species of duck which ranged in colour and size from the large white domestic variety to vividly coloured but small mandarin duck. They all quacked happily as they swam about catching insects.

I walked by the side of the lake, and along a gravel pathway that was covered with wysteria-twined lattice framework. After a while I came to a fork in the path. The right fork led to the part of the garden that contained a number of buildings designated as National Treasures and I decided to view them first. They were surrounded by beautifully designed woods and water gardens. The trees were resplendent in their autumn leaves of red, russet orange and yellow and the whole area was very pleasing to the eye.

I approached the first building through a tiled and decorated gateway. Outside each building there were notices giving a brief history and I was thrilled to see that there was an English translation to the notices. The first building was called Rinshin-Kaka, a villa which had belonged to the feudal lord of the Kish Province and which was, according to the history, the most important of its kind in Japan. It was built of wood and plaster and stood eighteen inches above the ground on stilts. There was a walkway running all the way round the outside of the villa that was covered by a sloping subsidiary roof. The main roof was thatched and had turned up edges supported by carved wooden eaves. There were many large windows especially on the side of the villa that overlooked a small lake, and these had heavy wooden shutters attached to them. Through the windows I could easily see the layout of the interior. Running around the inside of the house there was also a walkway in the form of a narrow corridor which was used to get from one room to the next, as there were no openings between the rooms themselves. There weren't even any doors between the rooms and the corridors but just sliding partitions which had paper walls and were highly decorated. The floors were covered with bamboo tatami mats.

The villa was constructed in three sections. The first consisted of four rooms, all on ground level. In the front was the room of Daisu, the room in which to prepare for the tea ceremony. The front interior room was called the room of the cranes because the sliding partition in it was adorned with painted cranes. The room on the left was the room of flowers and birds because the screens in that room were painted with flowers and birds of the four seasons. The remaining room of the first section was the room of Shosho which contained drawings of the eight beauty spots of Shosho, China. The second section of the building was designed and used for receiving visitors. This section contained only three rooms. The room of Juminoe; the room of Namura containing the ten odes of the Namura District written by nobles of the Imperial Court and; in the front, the room of musical instruments. The third section of Rinshin-kaka was built for the use of the wives of the feudal lord. It was the only part of the villa which had two floors, but each floor had only one room. On the ground floor was the dressing room of Yodo ginu, the wife of Hideyoshi Kano and the room above was called the room of Murasame.

As I walked around the little lake next to Rinshin-kaka, I passed a small wood and plaster building. It was only about twenty to thirty square feet in size and the front wall was in fact a pair of heavy wooden doors. The notice alongside the building explained that it was Tenzui-ji juto oido. An oido is a covered house and a juto is a kind of mausoleum erected during one's lifetime to celebrate its longevity. Tenzui-ji juto oido was three hundred and eighty years old and built in Daitoku-ji, Kyoto by Hideyoshi tokotami one of the greatest generals of Japan to protect his mother's juto from the weather.

The cover of the walkway matched the roof of the villa and the walkway had seats on either side of it. The path climbed upwards into the trees on the hillside and I followed it and walked among the backcloth of autumn colours and trickling streams. The trees hid a number of birds and their song filled the air. Halfway up the hillside I found a tea ceremony house Choshu-noka, which had been built by the Third Shogun, Imeitsu Tokugawa in 1623 in Nijo Castle, Kyoto. It had been dismantled and brought to Sankei-en gardens in 1932. The tea ceremony house was built of much thinner wooden planks than the villa and had a small balconied top floor and the upper floor had roofs on.

On the highest part of the hillside, but still completely surrounded by trees, was Gekka-den, the waiting room of the Daimyo who proceeded to Fushimi Castle. The notice said that Gekka-den was three hundred and seventy years old and was moved to Yokohama in the seventh year of Taisho, again from Kyoto. I couldn't help wondering why so many buildings had been moved from their original sites but could only imagine that the Japanese thought it sensible to distribute their National Treasures throughout the country so that they could be more widely appreciated. By the side of Gekka-den there were two small tea arbours. The structure and materials used were very similar to those of the villa, Rinshan-kaka, but the buildings were a lot smaller.

Nearby there was another building, also among the trees. It was Jizo hall, built on stilts with steps leading up to it. The conveniently placed notice explained that Jizo was the deity who, in Buddhist religion, was entrusted with the salvation of souls. Jizo hall was where the deity 'lived'. It was a plain building with only one roof and was a sharp contrast to the elaborate places I had just seen. It was said to be four hundred years old and had originally been built inside Shimpei-ji at Kakamura.

Shinso-ro was the next building to see. It was another tea arbour, much bigger than Choshu-koka and, although built of the same thin wood had a plain roof that didn't curl up at the edges. It was a kyoso-tei, nine-windowed arbour, and had originally been built near Gekka-den, three hundred and fifty years earlier. It was famous as an 'over three mats' tea arbour. It was much later that I discovered the relevance of the size of a mat. Apparently the Japanese rush mats or tatami are always the same size: six feet long and three feet wide. Every traditional house is built to include a number of mats, so that every three mat house is the same size; every four mat the same etc.

It was difficult to see the next building as it was hidden behind bushes and trees, and the path leading up to it was roped off, however I could see the description board and it read that it was Renge-en. It also stated that the mother of pearl column and the lattice work in the wall were from Hoodo hall. Unfortunately I couldn't see them though.

The more buildings I saw the more historical titbits I picked up, and the more fascinated I became about Japanese traditions and way of life. I was certainly beginning to appreciate the impressive heritage of the Japanese people and was determined to see as much of it as was possible on a short visit.

Renge-en was the last building in that part of the garden so I returned to the path around the big lake. As I walked towards the hill-top pagoda it began to spot with rain but the trees on the hillside provided adequate shelter. A steep path led up the hillside which was completely enclosed with trees at first and then a bamboo glade. The bamboo was so thick and tall that the path was quite dark, and looking upwards, I could see that most of the canes were oven twelve feet tall and some a good six inches in diameter.

At the top of the hill I came to a T-junction. The bamboo was so tall that I couldn't see the pagoda but I guessed correctly that it was along the left hand path. As I walked on the bamboo gave way to trees again. Their roots stuck up above the ground and every now and again I tripped over them! On either side of the path was a lattice work fence which, at first, I thought was made of wood but when I touched it to steady myself after tripping over another root, I discovered that it was an exceptionally good plastic imitation!

The pagoda was situated at the end of the path. It was unlike others I'd seen as its central column was completely built in. There were no windows or open galleries although there were some narrow walkways around the second and third floors. Each walkway was roofed creating the pagoda style, and each roof was curved up at the edges. The eaves underneath were decorated with carved faces. In the middle of the uppermost roof was the traditional spire-like rod consisting of a central 'stick' with circular bands positioned vertically up its length. At the top the bands formed into a double circle. The description board alongside said that the pagoda was a good example of Muromach architecture and it had originally been built in the compound of Tomyo-ji temple at Kyoto but moved to the gardens in 1941.

I retraced my route to the T-junction and went right where I found a concrete house which had been built to replace the house of Zenzaburo Hara, a silk exporter whose grandson-in-law had built Sanken-en gardens. The original house had, apparently, been the meeting place for famous Japanese painters and scholars until it was destroyed in World War II. The replacement house was ugly compared with the beautiful old buildings that I'd just seen, but from its upper floor there was a good view of Yokohama harbour.

It was still raining when I got back to the bottom of the hill and I had left the cover of the trees so I walked quickly, skirting the lake and taking cover in a small circular shelter. I was already quite wet but after about ten minutes it eased a little and I ventured out again. Not far from the shelter was Yokobue-an, the hermitage, where Yokobue had spent the tranquil remainder of her years after a famous love-affair with Tokiyori Takigushi. Yokobue had been a lady attendant at the court of the Empress Krenneimon-in and Tokiyori was a follower of Shingemori Taira, the Lord Keeper of the Privy Seal. The details board did not elaborate on the love affair but it must have been a sad one as it described Yokobue as a love-lorn lady. The hermitage was said to be eight hundred years old. It was very simple in design and built of wood. It had only one story with a thatched roof that looked like a bonnet, similar to thatch roofs on old English cottages.

I was glad that I was able to go inside the last building I visited, as the rain seemed to have set in for the day. It was a farmhouse and after paying an entrance fee of 50 yen at the gateway, I had a quick look at the outside before going in. A sign politely asked visitors to remove their shoes before entering so of course I did. A large board hanging on the wall in the first room gave details of the building. It was, apparently, built mid-eighteenth century by Susake Iwase, one of the richest men of Hida district, Gifu Prefecture. In 1960 it had been destined to be washed away as part of a dam construction plan, so the owner donated it to Sankei-en. The board explained that the left and right side of the building were quite different and that such a design was only observed in farm houses belonging to the upper class. Although the building was very large, equally as large as an old English farmhouse, and built of solid wooden logs, it was apparently built in the Gassho Zukun style and, as such, was held together without the use of nails or clamps. I was amazed by this information as it didn't seem possible that such huge timbers could be held together otherwise. The notice did explain, however, the method used and looking into the roof I could see it. Large logs called sasu, were stacked together like joined hands. The pointed ends of the sasu were then placed in little holes on a sasu receiver at the sides and the apex of the roof so that the weight was concentrated at those points and the roof kept in place. The joints in the framework of the building were held together with straw ropes or neso (dried young tree), which were the substitute for nails and clamps. Not only did the sasu receivers hold the logs in place but in the roof they also held a thick thatching of reed-like materials called miscanthus.

When I had read the notice I looked around the room that I was in. It was large and square and appeared to be the kitchen as, in the centre of the floor was a square pit which contained a log fire surrounded by the fine dust ashes of previous fires. Suspended on a chain above the burning logs, was a dumpy black kettle which hissed as steam poured out of its spout. There was no chimney, not even a hole in the roof, so the aromatic smoke just drifted around the room until it found its way out through the doorway or the roof. Along one wall there was a row of shelves and cupboards. The cupboards had sliding doors but these were open to reveal a display of lamps, sundials and chests. Hanging on the wall above the cupboard was an ancient-looking gun with a thin barrel, and in the corner of the room was a weaver's loom.

I had to negotiate a high step to get into the next room which effected a separation between the left and the right designs of the building. There were a number of small windows along the outer wall which were opaque. All of the rooms on this side of the house were similar with sliding screens between them and various built-in cupboards and drawers in the walls. There was a corridor running around the outside which could be used to get to the various rooms without going through them all. The floors were covered with the now-familiar tatami mats, and, above the sliding screens of the two largest rooms, there was a panel of decorated wrought iron, shaped to resemble a pair of ladies' fans. I walked through all the rooms, along the side, across the end and back down the other side of the house until I came to the high step back to the right hand side of the house.

The room I stepped down into was square and large, like the kitchen, and also had an iron receptacle holding a fire. There was a ladder leading upwards from this room into the left, but it was roped off. To the right was a doorway to the entrance where I'd left my shoes and I could see bundles of thatch material stacked up inside the entrance. Below the thatch was a large earth floored area that contained a farm implement like a chain harrow, and two wood and leather saddles. Leading from the room in which I was standing was a dairy and storeroom which contained a stone trough and various wooden barrels, pails, bowls, sieves, nets and casks. There was also a stone mill and, on the wall, a long piece of bamboo with holes in it used for hanging up spoons and ladles. I found all items on display very interesting and was surprised how a lot of the equipment was similar to that used in an old English dairy.

Even though I had been in the farmhouse a long time it was still raining. I put my shoes back on and returned to the lake. As I was about to leave the gardens, a throng of Japanese tourists arrived by coach to start a tour of the gardens. They were accompanied by two Japanese girls wearing blue uniform and carrying umbrellas. These were their guides. The bus was now several minutes walk, and I was drenched by the time the bus arrived. Several secondary school children were travelling home to lunch on the bus. They all wore smart blue uniforms: the girls in two-piece suits, a shaped blazer and a pleated skirt and the boys, straight-cut trousers and mandarin-collared jackets.

On nearing Yamashita Pier, the bus got stuck in a traffic jam, I was pleased as it meant I could stay out of the rain longer, but soon I was back in it. I decided that I should have no shelter from it at all as I walked back to the ship along the open quay, so I decided to go to the nearby Motomachi Shopping Street. It was a great disappointment compared to the one in

Kobe, with ninety per cent of the goods on sale imported, so when the rain eased a little I walked along to the Silk Centre to post some letters. The shops in the Silk Centre were all decorated for Christmas and packed with shoppers. At one of the entrances a stall was set up. It was a kind of tombola and each shopper was invited to have one free go. The tombola drum was painted red and had a small hole in one position on its circumference. When the handle was swung a ball dropped out through the hole. If a yellow ball dropped out you won a prize, but if it was red you didn't. I got a red ball!

Although the goods on sale in the Silk Centre were fairly expensive the quality was also good and I bought some Christmas presents there for my family which included a set of bamboo coasters, a handbag purse made of embossed paper that felt like material and contained a comb, tissues and a mirror, and a Japanese-style dressing table mirror.

I had decided to walk back through Yamachita Park where I had seen the crowds of happy picnic-ers on my first visit, but as I made my way to the traffic crossing, I passed the Yokohama Foreign Trade Advisory Institute, I noticed that a Christmas sale was in full swing. I have never been able to resist a sale so I went inside. The large hall was packed solid with stalls and people. The goods on sale were both foreign and Japanese and there were many crafts on display including carved figures; leather jewellery, woven baskets and wooden combs. Many of the stalls were filled high with clothes, ties, umbrellas, and coats and there were presents of every description. When I finally dragged myself away it had stopped raining. However, it was still bitterly cold and I walked quickly through the park. Previously I had only walked a short way into the park but now I discovered that there was a fountain with a large stone statue, the Guardian of the Water, in the centre, which had been presented to Yokohama by its sister city San Diego, California, U.S.A. There were flower beds all around the statue but because it was too cold for flowers the ingenious Japanese gardeners had used decorative cabbages instead. I had seen the cabbages on sale in the Motomachi at Kobe and had been impressed by them. There were two kinds, one, green with cream tinges; the other purple with mauve tinger. I walked right to the end of the park only to discover that I couldn't get out and had to retrace my steps back to the statue and, by the time I got out, it was raining again. The walk back to the ship seemed everlasting and I was aching and wet by the time I climbed up the gangway, but, after a short while of recuperation I was able to enthusiastically tell Colin of my day's exploits.

I didn't go ashore on our last day in Yokohama but was asked to put up Christmas decorations. There were boxfuls of decorations, which had been accumulated over the years, in a cupboard near the food store, so the Chief

Steward took me down to select the appropriate decorations. On the way we had to pass through the galley. It was the first time I had seen it. In the centre of the room there was an electric oven at least the size of two Aga cookers joined together. There was also a baker's oven which was even bigger. Below the galley was the food store It was a huge room with cupboards everywhere and a wired-off cage which contained row after row of tinned food. On the opposite side to that, the thick insulated doors of the refrigerated storeroom occupied a whole bulkhead. There were so many boxes of Christmas decorations that I was hard pressed to sort them all out, so, eventually, it was decided to take them all up to an empty cupboard opposite our cabin where I could sort them at leisure. It took all afternoon to search through the boxes and put up decorations in the bar, smoke room and dining room but afterwards they looked very gay. I even found two plastic Christmas trees which I put in the bar and decorated with fairy lights. By the time I had finished I was in a really Christmassy mood.

CHAPTER 15

KUDAMATSU, KANDA AND OUR DAY OUT IN KUKORA

Kudamatsu is situated on the shores of Honshu island, so our course from Yokohama took us around Shikoku island and up through the Inland Sea of Japan. It was a day and a half passage and we anchored off Kudamatsu at 3 p.m. on 15th December. We were called at 6.30 a.m. by the Mate knocking on the door and calling out 'Pilot on board!' which was Colin's signal to turn to. It was still dark and chilly outside, so instead of getting up I was able to lie in bed and look out of the porthole. We were anchored in Kasado Wan, a large bay almost completely surrounded by islands, which, in the half light were merely silhouettes. The sea was flat calm in the bay, and, as it got light, the trees on the islands were reflected in the water. Kudamatsu was just across the bay but all I could see of it was the scores of factories and on a hill behind, a number of high rise flats, the homes of the factory workers. There were only three wharfs large enough to accommodate ships but a number of smaller ones for the numerous coasters that plied in and out.

The pilot steered the ship straight for the nearest wharf, only turning and going astern at the very last moment so that, although it was a bit hair-raising, we slid perfectly alongside. The wharf was next to one of the factories and we learnt later that to get ashore we would have to go by liberty boat to the end of the second quay, as we were not allowed to walk through the factory premises, and, if we wanted to go ashore it was best to take a train or taxi to Tokuyama about six miles away as there was very little to see in Kudamatsu. I wasn't feeling too well when we arrived so I decided to stay aboard and spent an interesting time watching the comings and goings of the factory workers and the stevedores.

I was impressed by the layout of the factory. The buildings were all concrete and not very pretty but evergreen trees and bushes had been planted along the roadsides and around the buildings, effectively hiding them. By watching the numbers of workers going in and out I could see that they generally started work at 8.00 a.m. and finished at 4.30 p.m.

Before starting work, and in their lunch break, a lot of the employees lined up in rows and did exercises for about ten minutes. There seemed to be a set pattern of exercises as they all did the same one at the same time: bending; stretching; throwing their arms around and jumping on the spot, with great enthusiasm. They all wore uniforms of grey twill, buttoned through jackets with arm bands from wrist to elbow, and trousers, and some men wore white spats. The women factory workers had identical uniforms but wore short white pinafores over them. I learnt later that not only were the uniforms supplied by the owners but that also accommodation was subsidised, some children's schooling paid for and even holidays arranged and paid for, so it wasn't surprising that the employees worked hard because if they lost their jobs they lost everything.

The stevedores, being employees of the same firm, wore the same uniforms except the foreman whose suit was dark blue. They also wore crash helmets which had the inevitable green 'safety' cross on them. The foreman's helmet was bright yellow whereas the rest of the gang wore cream coloured ones. There was over one thousand tons of tin plate waiting to be loaded, when we arrived. The tin was in piles and each pile was packaged into a rectangle about two feet by five feet by three feet and had a protective cover of green polythene held on with strips of orange tape like a parcel. Shoreside cranes specially designed for lifting the parcels of plate, were used for loading. They were huge contraptions, at least a hundred feet high and standing on four legs, which fitted into runners so that they could be moved up and down the quay. The gibe of the crane unfolded over the ship's holds but instead of the gibe moving each time, the ropes and hooks were fixed to a cab which ran along the gibe. A man sat in the cab and worked the controls. He was able to see below him as the floor was glass. After a while he must have suffered terrible neck ache as he craned forward to see into the ship's hold.

The cargo was not stored on the quay but was brought to the ship's side on large twelve-wheeled lorries that had only half cabs. The organisation was so good that as soon as one lorry emptied another pulled up behind it. There was never a lorry waiting in queue but always one arriving as it was needed. The cargo was stowed in the holds using a fork-lift truck when the trucks were reversing they 'beeped' a warning, which to me, seemed a very sensible safety device. I'd also noticed such 'beepers' on Japanese lorries and vans. Besides making the noise the trucks at Kudamatsu had red revolving lights fitted on the back which flashed when they were reversing.

On one of my walkabouts on deck in the warm sunshine, I noticed that the water around the ship was full of jellyfish. They were a transparent pinky-white colour and looked like saucers, although their shape and circumference changed as they propelled themselves along. I watched them for a long time as besides a stray dogfish in Tokyo Bay, I hadn't seen any wildlife in the sea since leaving the Mexican coast. During the afternoon the weather deteriorated and, by the time we left at 4.30 p.m., it was spitting with rain. We sailed through the bay towards the one gap in the islands. The gap was very narrow and, as we passed through, the islands on either side looked a stone's throw away. Some small fishing boats were approaching the gap as we left and they rocked crazily in our bow wave.

The pilot who guided us out of Kudamatsu stayed on board until we anchored off our next port of call Kanda, three hours further up the coast of Honshu island. All I could see from our anchorage was the flashing light of the direction buoy but when it got light the following morning the hills surrounding Kanda Ko were easily visible. Kanda is situated on the most southerly of the Japanese islands, Kyushu and by consulting the chart I could see that we were just south of the narrow straits, the Shimonoseki straits, that divide Kyushu from the main island of Honshu where all our other ports of call had been. As we were taken into port we passed four large areas of land reclamation. Each was at a different stage of completion. The one nearest the town was finished but it only had grass growing on it. The other three areas, however, were still being reclaimed. One area was simply walled off and looked like a 'field' of water with a concrete fence around it but the other two 'fields' had what looked like three-legged stools of concrete positioned in rows, several feet apart. The legs of the stools were buried deep in the sea bed and the 'seat' was a huge cylinder of concrete which would act as a pontoon for concrete slabs and hundreds of tons of foundations. The foundations were obtained by quarrying a nearby hill and its stark face showed white against the surrounding hillside.

Alongside our allotted quay were hundreds of brand new multi-coloured pick-up trucks which were parked in rows waiting to be loaded onto a ship. They stretched for at least half a mile in every direction and behind them the Datsun factory where they had been made stood, tall and gaunt, watching over its prodigy. Out of interest, I made a quick count of the trucks, there were two thousand, three hundred and fifteen in all.

As soon as the gangway was lowered several gangs of stevedores swarmed aboard and before Colin had a chance to unlock the entrances to the holds, they had the cranes swinging into position. That afternoon the Third Engineer rejoined the ship with a completely healed little toe. He seemed very pleased to be back and especially to eat English food again. I had heard of the high cost of medical treatment in Japan but when he told us that his treatment was in excess of £1000, I was amazed. His room alone had cost 10,000 yen, about £50 per day!

The same afternoon a 'roll on roll off' car carrier docked in front of us and started to take on the trucks from the quay. The loading process was a really speedy one: a gang of drivers collected the trucks, one at a time, from the neat rows on the quay; drove them to the ship's side; then in turn, drove up a ramp that was fixed to the ship's side. At the top they turned at right angles; drove along deck and into a number of lifts positioned along the deck. The lifts transported them to the hold where they were lashed into place. The drivers then walked back down the ramp into a waiting minibus which took them back to the trucks on the quay and the whole process started again. A constant stream of vehicles boarded the ship during the afternoon and most of the evening, but the shop was still not full and no trucks at all were loaded the next day, Sunday. A number of officers had been on a car carrier before and they estimated that the ship could carry in excess of two thousand trucks in fact nearly all those waiting on the quay!

The stevedores didn't work our cargo the next day either, so Colin was fortunate enough to be free for the day. There wasn't much to see in Kanda but we were able to get a train to Kukora. The mate was also going to Kukora for the day so we walked with him to the small railway station. On the way we passed streets of rather ramshackle houses and a number of small shops.

We had to wait half an hour for the train and by the time it arrived there were scores of people waiting for it. As it was the last shopping Sunday before Christmas we knew there would be a lot of people about but we weren't prepared for the massive crowds we encountered during the day.

The seats on the train were already full when the train arrived and there was only a little standing room left. We felt a little cramped but not uncomfortably so ...until we arrived at the next station. There, however, more crowds waited. When they piled in we began to feel more overcrowded and we were jostled and prodded like a lot of sheep every time the carriage swayed or stopped. At the next station even more people were waiting and it took the combined effort of the people themselves, and the porters using hands and feet, to push everyone into the carriages. It was almost unbearable inside. People were squashing each other into ridiculous positions and I felt like the proverbial sardine in a tin! Between the first two stations I managed to get a fleeting glimpse of the surrounding countryside, small villages and green patchwork paddy fields, but now it was impossible to see, or do, anything! The train's movement was transferred to the passengers and as we lost our balance in unison, ripples of movement rushed down the carriages. At least some sensible passengers had opened the windows so it wasn't stuffy but as the train jostled and bumped along we became more and more uncomfortable.

Fortunately a few people got off at the next station before the next crowd got on, so the squash although not getting any better didn't get any worse. When we eventually reached Kukora everyone seemed to sigh with relief and as the doors opened we spilled out onto the platform. We were propelled along in a sea of Japanese people to the exits and only then were we able to catch our breath. It was a miracle that the three of us had managed to stay together but somehow we had and after a few minutes of recuperation, we shook ourselves out like battered flowers, and made our way to the shopping streets.

The Uromachi and its three accompanying shopping precincts stretched even further than the Isezachi-cho in Yokohama and the shops were crammed with Christmas offers and entwined with decorations. Throngs of shoppers wandered between the shops until they were laden with parcels. The majority of people were in family units and several women were carrying small children on their backs in harnesses. I did notice, however, that some of the men let their wives get on with the shopping and had escaped to the Pachinko houses which were packed, as usual, to overflowing. The constant clatter of the machines drifted out of the open doors as we passed by.

We spent a long time in a number of toy shops which contained not only vast arrays of moving and static cuddly toys but scores of ingenious cars, robots, horse racing sets, and building kits. These shops were a paradise for children and a fascinating pastime for us! I was so taken by the cuddly toys and by their relatively cheap price, Colin bought me a large floppy-eared sad-eye dog which we named Porky.

When we finally reached the end of the shopping streets we came across a market. It was a food market and after my bad experience in Taiwan we decided not to go any further. We wandered until our legs ached and then, after eating a hamburger and chips, we returned to the station. Again we had to wait for the train but this time it was far from crowded and we were able to collapse in comfortable seats and have a good view of the surroundings as they flashed past the window. There were quite large areas under cultivation unlike the built-up areas around Nagoya. The main crop appeared to be rice and the paddy fields were designed in tiers to facilitate flooding. The rice seemed to be in different stages of growth. In one field it was being harvested whereas in the next it had only just been planted. There were several villages and I noticed that the houses were quite modern and that several were still being built. All the houses were similar in design with the top floor smaller than the bottom one and covered by sloping roofs.

The return journey seemed far quicker than the earlier one and within twenty minutes we were back in Kanda. We caught a taxi back to the ship to save our aching legs, and arrived back on board the ship around mid-afternoon after an enjoyable excursion. Several of the lads were taking advantage of the day off and enjoying an afternoon in the bar so we joined them for a while until the beer ran out in the fridge and more had to be ordered. We left them to it then but we knew there would be a few sore heads in the morning!

As the next day was to be our last before two weeks passage to Mexico, I decided to walk into Kanda to get some last minute exercise. It was very cold at first but, as the sun rose higher, it began to warm things up and by the time I'd walked into town I was quite hot. It was obviously 'dustbin' day in Kanda as piles of rubbish were piled in the streets ready for collection. Later, I thought I heard an ice-cream van approaching but it turned out to be the dustcart playing a familiar tinkling tune to tell everyone of its arrival. The cart was very much like the ones used in England with an automatic feeder on the back but it was fairly small and another little lorry followed it around collecting the combustible waste which the householders had kept separate.

In town I bought a few last minute bits and pieces and had a look around one of the small supermarkets, which was remarkably like a small 'Mace' grocery store at home, with shelves of food, fridges full of prepared meat and vegetables and checkout desks. The Japanese ladies used wire baskets to carry their purchases but I didn't see any trolleys. By the time I got back to the ship, I felt I had had enough exercise for a few days. The Chief Steward had earlier asked if I would ice the Christmas cake so that afternoon I set to work. I hadn't iced many cakes before but I'd thought of an easy and appropriate design and after much fiddling and getting covered in icing, I managed to transfer a feasible copy of the design onto the cake! In the middle I had placed a large lifebelt, inside the belt I iced holly leaves and around the sides ship's bells. I put a few fussy decorations down the sides of the cake to cover the flaws in the basic white icing and finished it all by piping 'MV AMPARO 1977' around the lifebelt.

CHAPTER 16

OUR SECOND PACIFIC CROSSING AND CHRISTMAS DAY

The next day, December 20th, we set sail for Mexico although there were rumours that we may have to turn back to Yokohama for some more cargo. A lot of us hoped that we would be called back as it would mean Christmas alongside, but it wasn't to be and we spent Christmas Day in the middle of the Pacific Ocean.

December 25th dawned bright and sunny and the sea was nearly flat calm. Since leaving Kanda it had be constantly cloudy and the swell was enough to make the ship roll continuously, so we were all surprised by the fair weather conditions. Even though it was Christmas Day we went on as normal of course. The watchkeepers were called at the usual times. Everything was pretty quiet on the ship during the early part of the morning and I spent most of the time on the bridge. The sea was completely deserted except for a few faithful albatross and our nearest land was over eight hundred miles away (Wake Island) Although he tried, the radio officer couldn't even contact any other ships using morse and, like the roads in England on Christmas Day, the radio call-up frequency was completely silent. We were twelve hours ahead of GMT so in England it was still Christmas Eve and we thought of our families preparing for the following day.

After Smoko the Chief invited everyone for drinks in his cabin, although some of the lads had hangovers from the previous night. Everyone except the two watch keepers and the Chief Steward who was supervising the cooking of lunch, squashed into the Chief's day room to exchange 'Happy Christmas' and try to get into the festive spirit. It was obvious, however that people's thoughts were at home and we all agreed that Christmas was the worse time to be away from families. As Colin was on watch and I was the only wife on board, I was able to make myself useful by serving behind the bar, where we had a few drinks courtesy of the Shipping Company. The twelve to four watchkeepers had to have their

Christmas lunch early so that they could go on watch at the correct time but the eight to twelve watchkeepers and the Junior Engineers soon joined us and we listened to a tape recording of Christmas carols as we waited for our meal.

Lunch was set for 1.00 p.m. and when we arrived in the saloon the stewards were waiting to shake our hands and wish us 'Merry Christmas'. The tables were covered with sparkling white table cloths and there were crackers alongside each place. The menu looked very promising, a real feast, and as Christmas food was the only really Christmas event we could indulge in at sea we all looked forward to it with excitement. There were five courses listed on the menu: Menthe Cocktail, Asparagus or mushroom soup, crab duchesse with white wine sauce with smoked oysters, ham, turkey or steak chasseur; stuffing, cranberry sauce, sprouts peas, cauliflower, roast and lyonaise potatoes, and gravy, Christmas pudding and brandy sauce. Unfortunately the meal was a big disappointment. Apparently the cook had shown no enthusiasm and could not be encouraged to make any effort and the Pantryman wasn't much help as he had indulged in too much 'Christmas spirit' during the morning. Their combined lethargy resulted in four out of five courses being stone cold and the main course being minus a number of vegetables. Of course we all realised the extra work caused by the large and varied menu but the lack of effort had really spoiled the day and by the time we left the saloon the festive mood had dwindled away.

A few of us returned to the bar for a drink but soon everyone disappeared to their own cabins to sleep for the afternoon as there seemed nothing else to do. Around 6 p.m. a few people surfaced and made their way to the bar. A cold buffet had been laid on for the evening. The Cook and Pantryman had managed to prepare trays of cold meat and bowls of salad plus fresh fruit and my Christmas Cake, but it was the Chief Steward who made the best contribution to the day, he served up a beautiful dressed salmon. There were also some mince pies which had been bought in Hong Kong but unfortunately instead of containing the usual mixture of dried fruit, they contained minced beef!

When the eight to twelve watchkeepers left the bar for their watch there were only four of us left to celebrate Christmas night. We were not to be outdone though and stayed until midnight chatting and listening to music determined to make the most of an otherwise disappointing day. I hadn't really expected Christmas at sea to be anywhere near as enjoyable as Christmas at home, but after experiencing what it was really like I hoped I wouldn't ever have to spend another one 'aboard'!

We crossed the International Date Line the following day so we had two Boxing Days! We were able to say that 'tomorrow, yesterday will be today.' Shipboard life went on as normal and there was almost a feeling of relief that Christmas Day was over. The weather remained calm and sunny for several more days and although there was a strong headwind which lifted salt from the sea encrusting it onto the glass of the portholes. The Mate was really pleased that the weather had settled, as now the sailors could go out on deck to continue chipping and painting.

When we were only a few days sailing from Ensenada, the Radio Officer received a telegram from the agents asking us to go to Manzanillo instead of Ensenada. This meant that we had to alter course to the south and added two days to our passage. Time sped by for me, however, as, although I'd completed most of the needlework, I had with me I had a tapestry to complete and half the 'teach yourself Spanish' book to read and learn. About this time, however, I began to realise how I was missing female company and even though the lads were very sociable, I longed for a good 'natter' with another woman. It became warmer and warmer and New Year's Day passed by leaving a number of sore heads in its wake.

One evening , as we approached the Mexican coast another vessel came into view. It turned out to be a tug which was towing an oil rig. Colin called it up on the vhf radio/telephone and the watchkeeper aboard told him that his vessel was called the 'John Ross', the biggest tug in the world. They talked for a while and exchanged courses. The tug was on passage to somewhere in Texas USA. The tug was too big to pass through the Panama Canal so it had to go all round Cape Horn. The whole trip would take nearly three months.

As we entered warmer coastal waters our 'tail' of albatross disappeared, but soon their place was taken by squawking, spotted, seagulls and we knew that our passage was nearly over.

CHAPER 17

MANZANILLO; ACAPULCO; AND THE CRAZY LOBSTER

At 8.30 a.m. on 5th January 1978, we arrived at Manzanillo and the pilot boarded. It was seventeen days after leaving Japan. The sun appeared over the horizon as we made our way towards the breakwater but by the time we were tied up alongside the pier, about half an hour later, it was high in the sky and the temperature had risen considerably. On the way in I went on the Promenade Deck where I could see a lot of fish jumping out of the water. At first I thought they were jumping for insects but I soon realised that they were leaping about in a desperate attempt to escape from a large whale that was chasing them. He was swimming along with his mouth open taking in huge gulps of water and fish.

In true 'manana; manana' style it took two hours to start cargo discharge and although it was stated that we would be ready to sail the following evening, we all knew that we could add another twelve hours to that estimate. During the morning I did some sunbathing and it was lovely to feel the heat of an intense sun without wind caused by our forward motion. Before 11.00 a.m. the temperature had crept up to 85 degrees Fahrenheit. I didn't go ashore until after 3.00 p.m. because I knew that everyone would be taking their afternoon siesta between 1 p.m. and 4 p.m. and it would be like a ghost town in Manzanillo between those times. Cargo work had stopped as well and everywhere was quiet.

It was still very hot when I left the ship and, as I passed the sentry post at the dock gates, I noticed that even the guard was dozing in the shade. However, by the time I reached the main road a few people were emerging and as I followed the road along the coast I could see that there were a number of people on the beach and in the sea. I was quite tempted to go back to the ship for my swimming gear and join them, but when I remembered that the water contained poisonous jellyfish and sharks, I decided against the idea.

The trees that lined the main road looked even more withered than they had done on our previous visit and the 'moats' around them were bone dry. A wrinkled old Mexican man was passing by riding a donkey and leading to others. The donkey that he was riding was so small the man's feet nearly touched the ground on either side of it. The other two donkeys had large packs strapped to their backs. All three animals looked very scrawny and underfed and they plodded along wearily carrying their burdens. A little further on I had to leave the pavement to avoid rows of sharks fins that had been laid out to dry. They were covered in swarms of flies and although some of them were dry others looked as if they had just been placed there.

The town was as I remembered it: dirty, hot and dusty. The fountain in the plaza contained the same, green stagnant water but there were no birds on the wires, although I knew that at dusk they would be there again. It was nearly 4 p.m. and the sleepy shopkeepers were only just starting to roll up the metal shutters to open their shops. I walked the length of the high street. There were lots of people on their doorsteps chatting with each other sitting in the shade, or attempting to sell their goods which were laid out in front of them on the pavement. I walked on the shady side of the street as I could feel my arms and face burning in the hot sun. Colin had asked me to buy him a straw hat to wear on deck. There was a huge selection of hats in the 'Mexican Curios' shop and, in the end, I chose a smart 'cowboy' hat. I also went into a supermarket to get some paper handkerchiefs. The articles on the shelves were covered in dust and when I came out my hands were black with it. The return journey to the ship was just as hot as the previous one and I was tired as well as dirty by the time I got back.

The stevedores worked cargo throughout the night and Colin did the watch from 6 p.m. to 6 a.m. I slept as normal so the next morning I went out on deck while Colin caught up on some sleep. A dredger was working near our stern and the ship that had been moored behind us had left. Several fish were jumping for insects and the pelicans and seagulls hovered above them. It was a wonderful sight, seeing the pelicans diving for fish. When they had selected a target they pointed their heads and beaks downwards like arrows, then plummeted from the sky at amazing speed. They made a huge splash as they entered the water and the next thing I could see was the pelican floating back on the surface with a wriggling fish in its beak. They hardly ever missed.

During the morning we heard that another TMM ship was arriving at Manzanillo. She was the 'Josepha' and although she was on virtually the same run as us she was managed by a German company. It was decided that as she was going to Champerico, San Jose and Punteraneras, she would take the small amount of cargo that we had for each to save us going there. I was a bit disappointed that I was going to miss both Guatamala and Costa Rico, but some of the lads who had been there assured me that I wasn't missing anything and that both places were even more dirty and primitive than Mexican ports and that anyway we were still visiting Corinto and Acajutla which were just the same. The 'Josepha' arrived late in the afternoon and after taking on bunkers, she anchored out in the bay. It was arranged that we should leave our Champerico and San Jose cargo at Acapulco for her and she stayed at anchor until we left so unfortunately we didn't get a chance to go aboard her.

We finished discharging our cargo at midday on the Saturday, over a day behind schedule, then shifted to the bunker berth to take on fuel. We knew that it would take several hours to pipe aboard the large quantities of oil that we had ordered, enough to last for two months, so most of the officers and crew were able to relax and go ashore knowing there was no cargo to work and we wouldn't be sailing until the following morning. Colin was the duty officer for that night but the Mate stood in for him so we went for a stroll into Manzanillo.

It was a very humid evening. Groups of young people made their way to the Saturday night discos and dances, some already with their partners, others obviously hoping they would find one. The streets were packed with people in fact every person in Manzanillo seemed to be sitting on their doorsteps or walking in the street. Car horns hooted, happy people chatted and laughed as they wandered around and there was a general atmosphere of gaiety and vitality as they were all waking up after the lethargy of the day caused by the heat.

The plaza was a meeting place and acted as a starting point for the night's activities. Adults with babes in arms sat on benches around the square and children ran around the stone-flagged plaza. Every table with an umbrella was covetously occupied as it offered some protection from the birds, which were back in force on the telephone wires, transforming them into twittering, rustling rows of life. Some of the lads who had gone ashore earlier were sitting at one of the tables with an umbrella. They were enjoying glasses of cervesa (beer) and admiring the passing senoritas. We joined them for a drink and then had a wander around the shops amid the gay, humid atmosphere before returning to the ship.

We sailed for Acapulco at 8.00 a.m. the following morning. The sun was shining brilliantly and I sunbathed on the Monkey Island for an hour. I was glad that there was a breeze from our forward movement as without it, it would have been too hot to sit in.

We arrived at the Acapulco pilot at 1.30 a.m. the following morning. I woke up when the ship slowed down and went outside to see us in. We entered the harbour through a gap between two lines of cliffs. Once inside, I could see the crescent of Acapulco Bay. There were lights everywhere but I wasn't able to pick out anything clearly. It took nearly an hour and a half to get alongside and I got bored with waiting after an hour. Colin told me later that it was a wonder we got alongside at all as the pilot had been drunk when he boarded and spent most of his time staggering around the bridge wing. We had to drop anchor and tie up carefully as there was a strong swell even though we were in the harbour. This swell caused the ship to bump into the quay now and then.

I couldn't sleep very much that night, as I was too excited about going ashore in the famous Acapulco. When it got light I was up on deck to look around. The bay was very large with two lines of cliffs guarding the entrance. Almost all the buildings on the shoreline around the bay were high-rise hotels. Although they were concrete and modern they had been designed quite sensibly with balconies and decoration so they didn't look ugly or uniform. The two masses of land that skirted the entrance only had a few hotels on them. At the highest point on the left there was a large Monastery and a huge wooden cross. The right hand mass of land was reserved for the rich film stars and V.I.P.s that could afford to have a holiday home in Acapulco. There weren't many houses there but each one was very grand and had numerous terraces, swimming pools, balconies and patios. Behind our quay was a fort called Fuerte de San Diego, which had been built in 1616 to combat attacks from British pirates. At the time Acapulco was the chief Pacific port for the Spanish trade galleons that plied between China and Mexico. Between the fort and the next row of hotels were the shops.

In the same direction, but across the bay, I could see a number of game fishing boats tied up, each with a high deck and fixed chairs into which the fisherman strapped himself when hauling in Bonita, Barracuda, Sailfish, Yellow Tail, Red Snapper, Sharks, Amber Jacks or Marlin. The boats were for hire and for between $80 and $100 you could have the boat and equipment for the day. On the opposite side of the bay there was a Yacht Club where the private boats and yachts were anchored. There were scores of them with glistening white hulls and sparkling brass and chrome.

Again the stevedores worked around the clock to discharge cargo so Colin and the second mate decided to work twelve hours on six hours off six hours on and twelve hours off so that they could each have a free evening to go up the road. It was Colin's evening off first but I couldn't wait until then to go ashore but went straight away.

I decided to walk round part of the bay first before going to the shops. There was a wide promenade that followed the water's edge and passed the game fishing boats so I walked along that. At one place I passed a palm-covered area and a small beach and then came to a number of jetties. On the promenade end of each jetty billboards were posted advertising trips round the harbour and coastline. I don't know why, but these boats used were known as the 'Coca Loca' boats. Their Captains and crew were on the jetty touting for business, trying to sell tickets for their tours.

I noticed that the streets were much cleaner than the ones in Manzanillo and the surrounding area was well looked after. Besides the tourist's facade however, you could still see the dirt-floored shacks where the poor people lived and there were many unpleasant smells coming from the back of restaurants and cafes. Already, although it was only 10 a.m., music drifted from discos and restaurants and there were plenty of people on the streets. The inevitable hawkers were out in force carrying piles of leather sandals, hammocks, onyx jewellery; and a myriad of other goods and many were sitting on the pavements with their wares spread out in front of them. There were also a few blind and crippled people begging for alms.

I window-shopped for a while and then found the plaza which the local called the 'zocalo'. In Spanish zocalo means pedestal. Apparently in the days of the Spanish Conquest a pedestal had been erected in Mexico City to hold a statue of the King but in true Mexican fashion it had taken eighty years for the statue to be placed on the pedestal! The townsfolk used to say that they would meet at the pedestal and the word zocalo became known as the place of meeting and it spread to provincial towns.

At the far side of Acapulco's zocalo was a large Catholic cathedral which had a spectacular blue domed roof There were two white towers either side of large wooden doors at the front of the building. The doors were open and inside I could see rows of simple wooden pews. Light filtered through a number of attractive stained glass windows and candles flickered at the altar. I walked from the zocalo to the main street. I had been told that there was a 'Woolworth' store in Acapluco but I'd forgotten all about it so, when I was confronted by a large 'Woolworths' sign I was quite surprised. The shop was air conditioned and as I walked in, the coolness swept over me and I felt almost as if I'd leapt into a pool of cold water. I hadn't realised that it was quite so hot outside but now I could feel the sweat drying on my skin and I felt quite refreshed. 'Woolworth' was a self-service store with the familiar counters and pay desks. Most of the goods for sale were souvenirs or clothes but there was a large haberdashery department and cosmetics, perfume and medical department.'

After leaving the 'Woolworth' store I visited a few more shops where I bought two T-shirts with 'Acapulco' on them and on the way back to the ship I haggled with a hawker for Acapulco '78 beany hats. When I got back the stevedores were still working hard even in the tremendous heat. Colin told me that some of the gangs of men would be working all the time. It didn't seem possible for them to work the forty-eight hours it would take to unload, however, by sleeping during meal breaks and taking it in turn to have small siestas they continued working.

During the afternoon I watched various activities in the bay. There was something for everyone. Many were swimming and sunbathing on the beaches and there were people sailing, taking trips in motor boats, on pleasure cruisers, water ski-ing, riding on parachutes behind speedboats or just wandering around the shore in the beautiful sunshine. It was much hotter than it had been further north and I noticed that the locals had darker skins because of this.

Colin and I were both looking forward to our evening ashore in Acapulco so straight after the watch Colin changed and by 6.00 p.m. we were on our way ashore. It was still light but it was a bit overcast and in the distance we could see it raining over the mountains. Luckily, however, it didn't reach us. We made our way to La Quebrada, (the cleft in the rock) where the famous Acapulcan divers perform. We had to walk through the zocalo and past the cathedral. The zocalo was packed with people and we soaked up the wonderful atmosphere created by the heat and the Mexican's happy-go-lucky attitude to life. On the streets there were scores of women hawkers wearing peasant clothes; wide gypsy skirts; frilly blouses and checked lace-edged aprons. Some even had their children with them and if they were old enough they helped to sell the wares. Both mothers and children had bare feet and they were selling anything that they could: multi-coloured balloons, jellies, nuts, fruit and cold drinks.

From the zocalo we had to climb a steep hill to the Hotel Mirador which was built on the cliffs and commanded an excellent view of La Quebrada. Two of the engineers from the ship had beaten us to it and were sitting in chairs on the patio, sipping cold beers. We joined them at first but when we heard that the first dive of the evening wouldn't take place until 9.15 p.m. we decided to go and have a meal first. We both fancied the local speciality of lobster, so we asked a taxi driver to take us to a good 'lobster' restaurant.

The taxi, like most others in Acapulco, was a blue and white VW Beetle and we squashed ourselves into the back, and sped down the hill, along the narrow streets, past the Amparo, along the road that led around the bay with its rows and rows of hotels and finally pulled up outside a thatched stairway that led to Condesa beach. The name 'La Langosta Loco' (The Crazy Lobster) was written on a sign over the stairway. A smartly dressed man showed us down the steps and we arrived inside an open walled hut which had a thatched roof and was raised off the beach on stilts. There were fishing nets hanging from the roof, which, along with the candle illumination, gave a really romantic atmosphere. A waiter wearing a striped pinafore came up to us and showed us to a table for two. He could speak perfect English and he welcomed us to the Crazy Lobster, before recommending a drink of Crazy Banana Punch. He hoped that we would have an enjoyable meal and said that if we wanted anything just call for him – The Crazy Pedro! He went off to get our drinks while we perused the menu. We had already decided on lobster and when our drinks arrived, we ordered Crazy Lobster with a salad starter. The Crazy Banana Punch was delicious. It was a cocktail of fresh bananas, pineapple juice, orange juice and rum. The salad arrived soon afterwards, a great bowl of chunked tomato, lettuce, cucumber, green pepper and celery covered with thousand island dressing. We were not rushed at all but as soon as we had finished the next course arrived. It was carried on a huge tray above the waiter's head and placed with a flourish on a side table where it was served. Our Crazy Lobster course turned out to be two medium sized lobsters which had been boiled in their shells and then split in half and opened out, with fried rice and jacket potatoes. There were also bowls of melted butter which you could pour over the lobster meat. I hadn't tasted lobster before but after a few mouthfuls to acquire the taste, I found it very pleasant. The meat inside the shell was pinky-white and was moist and very tender. We ate our meal in comfort savouring every bite and luxuriating in our evening together. As we ate, a number if hawkers came along the beach and tried to sell us blankets and shawls. They displayed their goods on the thatched beach huts nearby. Later a fire-eater arrived. His act was spectacular and he blew out long jets of fire before dousing the fire sticks in his mouth. After his act he passed his hat around the restaurant for a collection. When we were ready to leave we complimented Crazy Pedro on the service and food and he was so pleased he rushed off and ordered what he called a 'sexy' drink on the house. We were delighted and sipped at the cold refreshing drink that tasted like whisked chocolate and coconut milk laced with a liqueur. I asked if he had a card so that I could recommend the restaurant to the others on the ship and he readily supplied me with a stack of visitor's cards and two free ash trays in the shape of Mexican sombreros with 'Crazy Lobster' written around the rim.

We left 'La Langosta Loco' in a very happy mood and walked a little way along the bay, past the hotels, and then got a taxi back to the Hotel Mirador. When we arrived the entrance gate was closed and an attendant said that it was 'residents only' for the diving. The lower, public observation platform was packed so I asked if, just this once, he would let us in. I wouldn't normally have dared but I had false courage after the drinks we'd had with the meal. To my surprise the attendant agreed. We just had time to order a drink before a man arrived at the top of the observation steps. He carried two flaming torches which flickered as he ran down the steps to the observation platform. When he reached it he hurled the torches against the cliff face, hopped over the wall and then jumped into the foaming water below. There were a number of swimmers already in the water and they took up their positions at the shoreline while the diver climbed up the rock face to the diving platform One hundred and thirty feet up on the facing cliff. Waves swept into La Quebrada from the Pacific and crashed against the jagged rocks. When the diver reached the platform, he looked out over the edge, and then turned and knelt at a tiny shrine of straw and glittery paper decorated with dolls. The hotel band, which had been playing jolly Mexican music, stopped and after a drum roll they started playing nerve-tingling music. The floodlights which had formerly illustrated the cliff and water below were switched off and everyone was given time for their eyes to re-adjust to the sudden darkness. The diver lit a fire and thrust two fire sticks into it. He held the burning sticks aloft, turning towards the hushed crowd. By now everyone was tense and excited and as if to ease the silence they all started to clap wildly. I could feel my heart beating excitedly. All eyes watched as the diver stepped off the platform and onto the edge. Because the water was not deep enough for the dive until one of the huge waves swept into the cleft, the diver had to time his plunge perfectly to avoid being smashed to pieces on the rocks. He waited for the correct moment and then launched himself out into midair in a perfect swallow dive. My heart leapt into my mouth, but, after what seemed ages, but was in fact only a few seconds, he entered the water perfectly amongst a foaming wave, and soon surfaced to a burst of clapping and cheering from the crowds. Almost immediately he was up onto the observation platform and was running up the steps so that he could get to the top before the spectators to collect donations from them whilst they were still luxuriating in the excitement of it all.

It was several minutes before my heartbeat returned to normal. We stayed at the hotel for another drink and when we left the diver had disappeared so we walked back down the hill to the Zocalo. There were a number of bars interspersed with shops and restaurants that lined the promenade so we strolled along towards them. At the second bar we found three of the lads from the ship. They had met up with two Welsh soldiers who were on holiday in Acapulco. They were stationed in Belize but had a week's leave so had decided to live it up in Acapulco. We sat down and had a few drinks with them. The Sparky, who had been on the Coca Loca boat trip that evening with one of the engineers told us what it had been like. Apparently as they toured around the harbour and along the coast to see the dive at La Quebrada, the drinks had all been free and a local band had been aboard to entertain them, he said they'd had a marvellous time. As we were sitting chatting, drinking our beers and Cuba Libras, a tiny Mexican boy who couldn't have been more than six years old, sauntered up to the bar carrying a wooden instrument like a barrel shaped maraca with rope wound tightly around it. He rubbed a stick up and down the rope to make a sound like a washboard. He lent casually against a nearby lamppost and while beating out a perfect rhythm on the instrument, sang an enchanting little song.

Everyone in the bar stopped talking amazed by the little chap's professionalism and skill. When he finished he graciously accepted the coins which we offered him and shoved them quickly into the back pocket of his shorts. As he walked away his shorts nearly fell off from the weight of all the coins!

We left the bar at 11.30 p.m. as Colin had to start the next morning at 6a.m.. We had both enjoyed our night up the road in Acapulco and slept like logs. I had a bit of a thick head and upset stomach the next morning which I accredited to the Cuba Libras. The headache soon started to wear off, however, as I ventured ashore again to see the daytime dive at La Quebrada. I had a quick look around the shops first and then climbed the now-familiar hillside. The dive was scheduled for 12.30p.m. and it was only 11.15 a.m. when I arrived so I was able to pick a good position on the observation platform. The sun was baking hot and after about half an hour I could feel it burning into my skin. There was no shade nearby and I was determined not to lose my good viewing spot. Some American tourists arrived wearing only swimming trunks and they climbed down to the water for a swim before returning to the platform to await the dive. Soon after that four or five Mexican boys got into the water and climbed a little way up the cliff to dive off as if they were practising for the big jump one day. After about half an hour one of the boys started to climb the cliff to the platform. As on the previous night he knelt at the shrine to pray and then walked to the edge. By that time the crowds had assembled on the observation platform and I had to lean forward to see the water below. A wave approached and the boy leapt out into the air. Again the dive was perfect and the crowds clapped enthusiastically. The boy climbed to the platform as if he'd just been for a swim and jogged up the steps to the top where he waited for contributions. As I handed him some coins I noticed that he wasn't the same diver as the night before.

As I made my way back down the hillside, the sun was still beating down savagely and my head started to ache again. I bought an ice-cream at a shop which cooled me down a bit and I was careful to keep in the shade on the way back to the ship.

I spent most of the afternoon watching the various activities in the bay and later the Sparky and I scrubbed the promenade deck.

That evening Colin didn't fancy anything on the dinner menu, so I went across to a restaurant called 'Hungry Herman's' to buy him a hamburger. As I walked up the quay I noticed a large motor yacht which had come alongside during the afternoon. It was a luxurious craft. On the poop deck there was a semi-circle of thickly cushioned settees and a man was reclining on them. He waved as I walked by.

'Hungry Herman's' was virtually empty but it still took them a long time to prepare the hamburger. While I was waiting I sat at a table near the door and watched the people walking by on their way to yet another entertainment. They were a motley assortment of people ranging from bikini-clad females swinging their hips, to fat gaily dressed men, swaggering under the weight of cameras and sweating profusely from the heat of the late evening sun. At last, the hamburger was ready and I hurried back to the ship with it, Colin assured me that it was well worth waiting for!

That was my last excursion ashore in Acapulco. The next morning at 6.00 a.m. we set sail again. It was still dark as we pulled away from the coast past a large passenger liner that was waiting to take our place at the quay. The sun began to show itself over the distant mountain tops and through the haze that hugged the coast I got a glimpse of Acapulco. I remember thinking how lucky I was to have had the opportunity to visit such a famous place and I knew that I would never forget it.

CHAPTER 18

CORINTO, CUTACO, ACAJUTLA AND MY ILLNESS

It was a two-day passage to Corinto, Nicaragua. The night before our arrival, however, I suddenly felt ill and went to bed nursing an upset stomach and muscles that felt like lead, I felt so awful the next day I couldn't have cared where we were and for the next two days I didn't leave my bunk. My whole body ached and my stomach was so delicate

I had trouble just drinking water. I had no idea what had caused the illness but I could only imagine it was food poisoning or sun stroke.

Apparently we anchored for a day off Corinto and didn't go alongside until the early hours of the following day January 14th. I didn't have the energy or inclination even to look out of the porthole until that evening when I eventually started to feel human again. I still felt very frail, however and didn't leave the cabin so I was only able to see the quayside and what appeared to be a small statue in the middle of it. We sailed that evening, at 8.00 p.m., bound for Cutaco, El Salvador, just a few miles up the coast. I had been out of bed all afternoon and by early evening my energy failed me and I went back to bed. The next morning I had to drag myself up but was determined to see us go alongside. I hadn't eaten anything for more than two days and my legs felt like jelly but as I couldn't see much from the porthole, after smoko, I ventured outside. Everyone seemed pleased to see me again which made me feel much better. From the deck I could see that we were tied up alongside a jetty which had a storage shed on it. There were two more sheds and a few office buildings at the other end of the jetty and a railway line stretched into the far distance where there was a village. Behind the quay there was a gently sloping hill, which, in spite of the excessive heat, was covered in bright grass and deciduous trees. There were no signs of the luxuriant growth of palms, bananas and rubber trees that I had expected.

I longed to explore the area but my legs would only take me a few steps and if my life depended on it I don't think I could have made it to the bottom of the gangway.

From the other side of the Promenade deck I could see that we were in a large bay dotted with islands. The islands were all stark and rugged, in contrast to the mainland. There didn't seem to be much wildlife in the vicinity except a few odd seagulls. There were no cormorants, pelicans, jumping fish, seals or dolphins as in other places we had visited.

It was tremendously hot outside. Whilst inside, in the air conditioned atmosphere, I hadn't realised, quite what it was like outside but at lunchtime the bridge thermometer read 100 degrees Fahrenheit and although it wasn't humid it felt like being closely surrounded by electric fires. I felt sorry for the people who had to work in such temperatures but realised that the stevedores were quite used to such extreme heat which they experienced all year round. They manhandled the cotton bales that we had loaded hour after hour and although the sweat rolled off them they didn't seem to tire. They didn't protect themselves from the sun and wore only loose cotton shorts and pieces of cotton material wrapped around their heads to keep the sweat out of their eyes.

During the morning several of the locals and their families walked out to the quay to have a look at the ship. They were all well dressed and looked amazingly cool in the blistering heat. I was very disappointed to have 'missed' Corinto completely and to be unable to go ashore in Cutaco but I learnt a bit about them from the lads. They said that at Corinto they hadn't been much to see and that if you stood in the little square that I had seen from the ship and turned through three hundred and sixty degrees you would have scanned the whole of Corinto. There had been no shops but several stalls lined the road from the quay to the square. They had been made most welcome by the local 'ladies' who, according to the Admiralty pilot Book no less, were renowned for their beauty. Apparently there had been a small brown piglet rooting about untethered near the bar where they were drinking. Knowing of my fondness for pigs they had contemplated catching it and bringing it back for me as a 'get well' present. Luckily , at the last minute, they had decided against the idea. I couldn't help laughing as I imagined them running back to the ship carrying a squealing piglet, but I was very touched they'd thought of me.

At Cutaco the stevedores worked all night and we sailed at 7.00 a.m. the following morning. As we were leaving the bay I finally saw some wildlife. There were about a dozen pelicans diving excitedly for fish. They didn't stop to eat the fish but instead quickly stored them in their pouches and dived again for more. While the crew were storing the mooring ropes on the poop deck more wildlife was discovered. This time it was a rat. It had found a secure hiding place under a winch and although they tried everything to flush it out, they couldn't catch it. I hope that it would be caught and killed quickly as the thought of a rat in our cabin made my skin crawl. Strangely we never saw it again and there were no reports of it having been caught.

I went on the bridge during the morning and was amazed to see that the temperature was 120 Fahrenheit in the sun, however, it wasn't really uncomfortable as it was a dry heat and there was a breeze caused by the ship's movement. During the morning I saw a number of giant turtles paddling along on the surface of the water. Every now and then they lifted up their rounded heads and swivelled them like periscopes. There were also the occasional dolphins. They were in very playful mood and as our wake washed over them they leapt into the air as high as they could, and then relaxed completely, splashing back among the waves with a resounding belly flop. Colin said there was a reason to their actions, as when they hit the water any parasites clinging to them were forced off.

We anchored off our next port, Acajutla, for four hours. From our anchorage I could see that the town was situated on a long, flat, plain which stretched from distant, still-active volcanoes to the shores of the Pacific. The banks of the plain were only about twelve feet above sea level. The whole area was covered with course grass and a large thick mangrove swamp lined the shore. In one place, close to Acajutla itself, , the plain ended, not abruptly as elsewhere, but in a slightly slanting beach of grey, volcanic sand. At the back of the beach, along the limits of the mangrove swamp, I could see a number of very primitive huts which were in fact home for the locals. The huts had domed roofs and were thatched and their walls appeared to be cemented with mud. Scantily-clad children played happily around the huts and on the beach. I couldn't see clearly the main part of Acajutla, because it was hidden by the luxuriant growth of the mango trees and coconut and banana palms, but I knew that it was only a small place with less than 3,500 inhabitants. There was no harbour as such, but a breakwater jutted out from the bank of the nearby plain. The breakwater was described on the chart as the new pier. The old pier was built on the beach and was just a row of flimsy posts which held a rotting jetty and two wooden storage sheds. When we went alongside the new pier, however, I could see that it was well supplied with modern loading equipment. There were two large tugs which guided us alongside and on the breakwater were forklift trucks, lorries and even an expandable gangway which fitted neatly onto the ship. The gangway needed to be expandable because there was no protection in the form of a harbour. The waves came straight in from the Pacific and the ship moved freely up and down the quay.

I still hadn't fully recovered from my illness so I went to bed early. We were only alongside for seven hours while the ninety tons of cargo we had for Acajutla was discharged. There was no cargo to be loaded there so we sailed at 6.00 a.m. the following morning.

The two and a half days passage back to Manzanillo was very pleasant. I slowly regained my former health and was able to catch up on a pile of washing, ironing and letter writing that I had neglected. The temperature hovered around 90 degrees Fahrenheit and I sunbathed every day and had the best suntan I'd ever achieved. The coastal waters were filled with wildlife and we saw dolphins, turtles and were followed by birds of every size and description. Some of the lads even saw a Manta Ray floating near the surface. Several times, mainly early in the evening, we saw huge shoals of fish jumping for insects. There were so many that their combined mass of bodies darkened the sea and as they jumped they shone silver in the sunlight.

At sunset, on the eve of our arrival in Manzanillo, we passed Acapulco. We were only about eight miles away so we could easily pick out the lights of the airport, monastery, hotels in the bay and even Quebrada through binoculars. The sight of Acapulco seemed to fill everyone with excitement again and memories of the good times we had had there. Instead of going in the bar we took our chairs out on to the Promenade Deck and the electrician rigged up a tape deck so that we could listen to 'Golden Oldies' as we watched Acapulco disappear into the darkness.

CHAPTER 19

MANZANILLO, MAZATLAN & THE CANADIAN COUPLE

When we arrived at Manzanillo on the 19th there was no berth or cargo for us, in fact, according to the apologetic agent, there were no definite plans for us at all. We anchored in the bay and waited while Mexican bureaucracy sorted itself out. It took the rest of the day and until 6.00 a.m. the following morning. The port was very busy and there were other ships at anchor besides ourselves. When a passenger ship arrived early that morning, one of the cargo ships had to be moved from the town pier to allow it to go alongside.

The passenger ship was the P and O Pacific Princess, which although registered in London seldom returns to England and most of the time plies between America and Mexico. It was a very smart ship with many promenade decks and swimming pools and the whole of the after-end superstructure block was glass. There were a fair number of passengers lining the rails but she didn't seem to be fully booked. The passengers were only given time for a quick look around and at 2 p.m. the Pacific Princess left for Acapulco.

Again, the area around Manzanillo was teaming with wildlife. In the morning I watched a small pilot whale chasing fish around the ship and in the afternoon, on one of my regular walkabouts on deck, I saw a large flock of pelicans, about sixty birds, flying in 'v' formation. The leader set the pace and he stopped flapping his wings the others stopped, in turn, down the line, like 'Tiller Girls' doing high kicks at the London Palladium. There were so many of them that by the time the last one had stopped, the leader was flapping again and so a continuous ripple of movement spread down the lines of birds.

They flew over the bay and the ship still in formation, but when they got over the hills behind the town, they started to spiral still following the leader whose beak was almost touching the tail of the last bird as he circled. They went round and round until the formation got very jumbled and the leader broke out of the spiral and back to the 'v' formation. Soon afterwards they split into two groups and headed off in separate directions, the larger group going south and the smaller one north.

When we eventually went alongside, there was a frantic rush of information and the poor Mate only had a few minutes to work out the cargo figures. There was no cotton as it was the end of the season, but quite a lot of other cargo had been found and included lead; shoes; curios; and barrels of seaweed.

We were again berthed as far as possible from the town but I walked up the road next morning and enjoyed the exercise. It was very overcast and the sun was completely hidden which made it quite cool and very pleasant for walking. There were only a few people in the streets but the hawkers were out in force again. My Spanish by this time had considerably improved but I found that writing and reading in Spanish was far easier than speaking it. It was quite enlightening and satisfying, however, to find that I could read notices and shop signs quite easily. There were numerous signs that had meant nothing before but now I could understand them. Two of the signs I found especially interesting. One was nailed to a huge heap of rusting buses and cars on the roadside. It said 'I buy old iron' which was really quite obvious but which I hadn't even guessed at before! The second was daubed on a bridge near the centre of town and was quite touching. It read 'To love children you must understand them.'

I searched diligently through the dusty shops to find some embroidery silk which I needed to complete a blouse I was making for my niece. Eventually I ran some to ground in a toy shop! I had a swift walk around the high street and then returned to the ship in time for lunch.

We were all, by that time, used to the delays and alterations of our schedule so we weren't a bit surprised when our stated departure time 6 p.m., stretched to 11.00 p.m. Before leaving we all had to check in with the Immigration Officers, presumably to prevent anyone jumping ship to stay in Manzanillo. It seemed strange that the checking only took place in Manzanillo and Ensenada and not in other Mexican ports and I felt sure that all the passengers off the Pacific Princess had not been checked. After all, as one of the lads put it, who would want to stay at Manzanillo, after they'd just left Acapulco?

Our hop up the coast to Mazatlan only took a few hours and we arrived there at 4.30 p.m. the next day. As we approached the harbour, several shrimping boats were leaving. They had long booms which were stowed vertically over their decks but which were extended over the sides to hold the nets when fishing. The boats had very brightly painted hulls and superstructure and bobbed along merrily towards the fishing grounds.

The town of Mazatlan is built on a rugged peninsula which juts out into the sea. The surrounding area is quite flat, the nearest mountain being far away in the distance but at the coast large cliffs rear up as if to defend the town from encroaching water. The harbour is behind the town and gained through a channel, which is, in fact, the widened estuary of a river. The mouth of the estuary has a man-made breakwater running across it with a small gap left for access. There were several luxury yachts at anchor in a small inlet which we had to pass to get to our berth. A ferry terminal for the La Paz ferries was sited behind the inlet.

As we slowly made our way up the channel, I could see that the town followed the coastline along the peninsula and on the opposite side of the channel, behind the cliffs, there was a lagoon which held some of the estuary water. When the agent boarded we heard that no cargo was being worked that evening and as it was the Second Mate's night on board, Colin and I decided to go up the road. It was dark by the time we left the ship and as we walked along a wide avenue towards the town, we could see that the evening meal was in progress.

The town, as usual, was centred around the Cathedral and Plaza and as we had been able to see the Cathedral's spires from the ship we easily found the town centre. The streets, were crowded especially around the numerous street stalls that lined the road. The Plaza, of course, was also crowded and full of hawkers and shoeshine boys. In the centre of the Plaza was a decorative bandstand and this was surrounded by a liberal scattering of multi-coloured streamers which radiated outwards like a cobweb, to the trees and benches at the periphery. The Cathedral overshadowed the whole area. It had twin spires which towered above a domed roof. Both the spires and the dome were painted gold.

We followed streams of people who were making their way to the seafront and soon reached the coastal side of the Peninsula where Pacific breakers foamed up a curved sandy beach. Along the front were a number of hotels but fewer than I had expected in a popular holiday resort like Mazatlan. We walked along a wide promenade past teenage couples romantically staring out to sea and groups of giggling girls being watched by groups of gangling boys.

After walking to the headland we returned to the hotel area where we found a convenient open air bar. We sat down next to an American man and when a thin moustachioed Mexican waiter arrived we ordered two beers and a plate of camerones Rancheros (shrimps in garlic sauce). I decided, although tempted by the menu, to steer clear of shoreside food until my stomach had completely recovered. We chatted casually to the American who like most Americans we met told us proudly of his connections to England, the Fatherland. It turned out to be that he wasn't an American national after all but had been born in Germany. He had to admit, however, that he had lived in America for more years than he cared to remember. He was joined by a couple from Canada. Their home town was Vancouver. They were both of retirement age and extremely friendly. We chatted enthusiastically and I realised that, at long last, I had an opportunity to have a good 'natter' with another woman. They had been in Mexico for a month and had visited Mexico City, a small settlement in the mountains and Acapulco before returning to Mazatlan. We swapped stories of our travels and talked of our homes and relations and eventually the subject got round to politics and economics in our respective countries. We talked as though we had known each other for years. The American left us after a while to finish his packing as they were all leaving for home the following day. We ordered another round of beers and from time to time, the waiter arrived with free Tequila, as well as the beer. We learned from Jack and Sue, the Canadians that there was a special way to drink Tequila. Apparently one should first put a slice of lemon in your mouth, drink the Tequila through the lemon and then quickly eat some rock salt which was always supplied with the drink. Even drinking it the 'proper' way, I couldn't find it palatable, in fact it resembled neat paraffin, however, Colin found it quite pleasant. The mixture of beer and Tequila had a marked effect on his speech and at one stage, I wondered if I might have to carry him back to the ship!

After a while Sue and Jack kindly invited us back to their hotel room for a drink. We didn't have far to go as their Hotel was next door to the bar. We walked through the open reception area and past a large central Patio which had a clear blue swimming pool in the middle of it, surrounded by a number of shady trees. Their room was on the fifth floor which we reached by lift from the Patio. All the corridors were wood panelled and their room was large and airy. They also had a balcony that looked over the bay, so we took chairs outside and sat listening to the breakers rolling up the sands and bursting amongst the rocks.

We weren't silent for long as there seemed so much to tell each other. I was especially interested by Sue's account of a local wedding they attended at a small ranch in the mountains. The groom, a young lad of 16 and his bride, who was slightly older than him, had been married in the tiny local church. The groom had worn a smart black suit with a frilled white shirt and large bow tie and the bride's dress had been white, very frilly and highly decorated with ribbons and bows. Afterwards the reception had been held in the open yard at the ranch, amongst the chicken and next to the cattle corral. There had been plenty of drinking, eating, laughing and music and dancing although the guests didn't bring presents they had to pay for a dance with the bride or groom by pinning notes of money on their respective partner's clothes.

We talked on and on , not realising the time, until Colin realised it had gone midnight! He had to be up early next morning to do the cargo watch so we reluctantly took our leave. We had already exchanged addresses and promised each other that if we were ever in visiting distance of either home we would 'drop in'. As Colin's company have ships which regularly call at Vancouver we felt that we may meet again some day.

We hailed a taxi from the street outside which took us back to the dock gates and then we wound our way back to the ship and managed to arrive in one piece although I almost broke my ankle when I fell in a hole that was unlit and unmarked!

The next day Colin had a hangover, but amazingly I felt fine and by 9.00 a.m. I was on my way back up the quay to visit the town. In daylight I could see that the Avienda (Avenue) which we'd walked down the previous evening, was lined with coconut palms and a selection of oily-leaved trees. Some of the trees had brightly coloured flowers on them but others had long seedpods hanging from their branches. The streets were fairly clean so I was surprised to see more flies than I'd seen in any other Mexican town. There were hundreds of thousands of them swarming around the trees and sitting on the pavement.

The houses lining the 'Avienda' were very tidy and built of brick and plaster in the Spanish colonial style. They had shady patios filled with green pot plants and screened by decorative wrought iron fences. The windows were barred and had thick wooden shutters to shade the rooms from the intense midday heat. Several even had small lawns between the house and the pavement.

I had decided to return to the beach first to take some pictures and when I arrived there, there were scores of schoolchildren walking along the promenade and sitting on the walls waiting for the nearby Secondary school to open. They all wore smart uniforms: the boys trousers and shirts; the girls skirts and blouses. There were four schools in the surrounding area and each had different coloured uniforms.

By this time the sun was high in the sky and extremely hot so the sea looked very inviting. I walked along the promenade again and then strolled back through many narrow streets to the town centre. On the way I passed one of the schools which was then open and alive with the noise of laughing chattering children.

Once in the town centre I was surrounded by people. Many housewives were doing their daily shopping and tourists browsed in and out of the souvenir shops. The Zocalo was also crowded and the shoe shine boys still busy, I stopped to buy some postcards from a temporary stall which was laden with everything from matches to silver earrings. The food stalls which had been so popular the night before were still at the roadside full of oysters; octopus; shrimps; fresh fruit; sweetcorn; tortillas; tacos and hot dogs, but this time they were virtually deserted.

Close to the cathedral I was surprised to find a market. It was completely covered and divided into sections, each for a different commodity. On one side there was the souvenir and clothes stalls which were partitioned off from one another and piled high. In the centre of the market there were the grocery stalls, again partitioned apart. Shelves were joined to the partitions and each shelf packed solid with tins and packets and boxes, every type and colour imaginable. The meat section was next to the road that passed the Zocalo and the front area was covered with fruit and vegetables. There were no fish stalls to be seen. I imagined that there was a separate fish market nearer the harbour. The goods, as in most markets, were cheaper than in the shops. I bought a large jar of tomato juice for 12 pesos which in the shops would have cost 15 to 20 pesos.

The market was crowded with people, the souvenir area with tourists, the rest with busy housewives and their trail of children. The fruit and vegetables looked very appetising, but there was a rather unpleasant smell coming from the meat section, so I didn't linger.

After a wander around a superstore which advertised a sale, I returned to the ship soaking up the beautiful Mazatlan sun as I went.

CHAPTER 20

GUAYMAS AND THE LIFEBOAT EXPEDITION

We sailed on time for once at 5.30 p.m. and left the harbour along with a small flotilla of shrimp boats.

The next morning we woke to find that a strong, rather cold wind was whipping the sea into a frenzy of waves fifteen to twenty feet high, which caused the ship to shudder and pitch. During the day it got worse. I was quite pleased when we arrived in the lea of cliffs at Guaymas and awaited the pilot. He didn't arrive, however but sent a message to say that he would be taking us in the following morning, so we had to anchor overnight.

As night fell the temperature dropped dramatically and outside it felt quite wintry. The air conditioning still poured out cold air and I had to put an extra blanket on the bed before I could get warm enough to sleep. When Colin was called next morning at 6.30 a.m. I couldn't force myself to leave the nice warm bed and I didn't emerge until we were alongside. It was bitterly cold compared with the temperatures we'd recently been experiencing but the sun, which was rising, promised to warm things up a bit later in the day. There was no mail awaiting us which was a little disappointing as we'd only received one letter since leaving Japan. The agent brought news, however, that from somewhere they had found seven thousand bales of cotton and considerable amounts of sesame seed which would take four days to load.

I went up the road at 9.00 a.m. as I knew that it was at least a mile to the town and it would take me quite a while to walk. The road between the dock gates and the town was paved but only with a mixture of sand, rubble and pieces of concrete and in places it petered out into a mud track. The houses along the roadside were very tumble-down although far superior to the tin shacks perched precariously behind them on the mountainside. There was a school on the roadside not far from the dock gates and I was amazed how it closely resembled a prison. The windows were all barred, the glass in them cracked and broken and the walls were covered in graffiti. The schools in Mazatlan had not looked very inviting but this one looked terrible.

As I walked towards the town, I had to pass groups of men lounging around outside the houses as though they had nothing else to do.

As I passed they not only stared intensely, undressing me with their eyes, but called out obviously lewd remarks in Spanish interspersed with "Hi Bonita" and in English "Hello Darling!". It was most embarrassing and my embarrassment turned to fear when one group of men tried to get me to ride in their car under the pretext of giving me a lift into town. I just walked on and they didn't attempt to stop me but by the time I arrived in town I was seething with anger at the baseness and lechery of the Mexican men, although I realised that it was probably my own fault for going ashore alone.

The town had two squares, One obviously the local Zocalo which was outside a large white church. The other a show piece for visitors which sported three high statues of Mexican presidents. There were, in fact, statues everywhere. Some were of local dignitaries, others of trade union leaders. One of the statues, however, was older and more pleasant to look at. It was of a rugged man who wore a large hat. He was sitting on a rock with a large writhing fish entangled under one of his legs. This statue was the 'Fisherman's Guardian' and he sat proudly on a rocky jetty overlooking the numerous fishing boats that trailed in and out of the harbour.

The main street of Guaymas was lined with large modern shops which were glass fronted and clean looking and even the shops on the side streets were modern. Behind the main street I found an undercover market that was so crowded with stalls that the walkways between them would only accommodate one person at a time. There were many vegetable and grocery stalls and a number of souvenir and commodity stalls all jumbled up together. I forgot my anger as I browsed around but even here the men looked at me as though I had two heads!

In several of the shop windows I noticed posters advertising the local annual Carnival which was due to start the following day. The posters advertised singers, dancers and matadors for a bullfight. Preparations for the Carnival were in full swing. Two grandstands were being constructed on a piece of wasteland in the high street and streamers were being tied between lampposts and across streets.

When I returned to the ship, I walked on the other side of the road, next to the railway that led to the port. There wasn't a pavement on that side but it meant that I could avoid the rude comments, if not the stares, of the men on the other side. The walk wasn't very pleasant, however, as now and again I had to pass the fly-infested body of a dog or a fish which had been idly thrown next to the railway line.

The sun, true to its promise had raised the temperature to above 80 degrees and even though I'd taken off my jumper and rolled up my shirt sleeves, I was baking when I eventually got back to the ship.

The stevedores at Guaymas did not work nights so it meant that Colin had a lot more free time and the next morning he was able to come ashore with me for a look around. This time, as we walked to town, there was no comment from the men still lounging at the roadside, but they still stared unabashed. The Carnival preparations were again in full swing but the grandstands weren't finished and didn't look as if they would be! Around the 'show piece' square a fair was being erected. The equipment, however, looked very antique and the dodgem cars and roundabout were rusty and frail looking. We didn't stay long in the town but it was pleasant to have a browse before returning in a taxi.

After lunch the Second Mate suggested we lower the lifeboat for a drill and to take it around the bay to ensure that it was working to regulation standards. The engineers were all working but Colin wasn't due on cargo watch until 2.00 p.m. and the Sparky also agreed to come with us. The Captain was in favour of the idea and so we all gathered on the starboard side and prepared to lower the boat. It took over half an hour and everything went wrong! Wires became trapped, handles were difficult to remove from corroded holders, winches didn't work in at least two places and, as the boat was gingerly lowered the rudder hit against one of the deckheads and the tiller arm broke against a metal bar. Eventually, after a hurriedly made up tool kit was produced to replace the one that didn't seem to be in the boat, or in a store where it was supposed to be, we all got into the boat and were lowered into the water. All the difficulties experienced prompted us to ask why the boat wasn't lowered every week at fire drill practise. Of course, this caused black looks all round but it was explained that boats had been lost while lowering them at sea and so the practise was stopped.

Once in the water, everything went smoothly, the engines started first time and soon we were chugging along past a nearby island, startling the birds that bobbed on the surface. The propeller churned out a little bow wave and my spirits soared.

We had to return to the ship after a short while and drop Colin off in time for him to do the cargo watch but then we made our way across the bay to the town. We passed another island on the way and we noticed a small shrine (that looked like a bus shelter!) nestled against the rocks above one of the beaches. We also had to pass the fishing boat quay and its adjoining fish factory. There were rows of pelicans sitting on the roof of the factory waiting to swoop on unattended scraps. The sun was beautiful and because we were so close to the water it smelt fresh and salty. By the time we reached the jetty which held the statue of 'Fisherman's Guardian, twenty minutes later we were all in a happy carefree mood.

The Second Mate steered us alongside perfectly and after tying up stayed with the boat while the Sparky and I found a shop that sold ice-cold beers. When we got back three small children were at the end of the jetty staring intently at the boat with eager eyes. I smiled at them and their dark eyes twinkled back at me.

We had a cold beer each and put the others in a bucket of cold water to keep them cool, before casting off and rowing out into the bay again and along the coast. The far edge of the town, next to the water, was obviously the high class area. The houses were very luxurious and all of them had a number of balconies, patios and well laid out lawns and shrubberies. Looking further into the distance, however, we could see the marked contrast in standards of living as scattered on the mountainside were the more familiar tin shacks that house the scores of poor families. As we followed the coast around we arrived at a small inlet which ended in a muddy estuary. The inlet was crowded with pelicans standing in the mud. We disturbed their afternoon siesta and several of them took off noiselessly to fly inches above the boat.

After chugging along for several more minutes we noticed a group of thatched buildings in the middle of a sandy beach. I had seen the words beach........bar.......beach casually marked in pencil when I had looked at the chart of the area earlier. Sure enough, as we got closer we could see that the building did in fact house a bar. We couldn't resist the temptation to go alongside so we shipped oars and approached the beach.

The bed of the bay was mud and sand so there was little danger of 'holing' the boat but even so there were a few rocks around and we decided to pole our way into the shallows using the boat hooks. This, we thought would be easy but it proved impossible because of the tide and the thick oozy mud, so in the end, we had to start up the engine again and chug slowly forward until we were close enough for Sparky to jump over the side and pull us in. The Second Mate tied the little ladder over the side so that we could get back in later and then he too jumped into the water. By this time Sparky was tying the boat up to a convenient rock on the beach. I couldn't help feeling like a castaway on a desert island! The Second Mate had gallantly offered to carry me on his shoulders so that I wouldn't get wet but being my clumsy self, as I was climbing over the bows I got my foot caught in the rope and went head first into the water. I was drenched to the skin and very cross at myself but as I stood up spitting dirty water we all saw the funny side of it and doubled up laughing!

We were still laughing when we ordered some drinks at the bar but we were amazed to see the bar tender had a straight face and looked as if he was completely used to lifeboats beaching outside his bar and its occupants flailing about in the water.

This made us laugh even more. Besides the bar and adjoining shack, the beach was deserted although a few children played on rusty swings nearby a road passed close to the beach leading into Guaymas. We wandered up the beach and had a swing and I flapped my arms around trying to dry off. The sand was hot underfoot and every now and then we stepped on sharp three-pronged thorns which were buried in the sand. This made us howl with pain each time we did it. It was nearly 4.00 p.m. by the time we clambered back into the lifeboat and by then I'd dried off. We weaved our way back to the ship around the islands and found that getting the boat back onboard was infinitely easier than lowering it! Soon I'd had a hot shower and we were relating our exploits to the others. They also thought my 'swim' was hilarious but I didn't mind and I laughed with them.

The next day we heard the shocking news that one of the company's ships had officially been reported missing with all hands. She had been on passage between America and Mexico when radio contact was lost whilst she was in the infamous Bermuda Triangle. The U.S.A. coastguard had made extensive searches but only a small amount of wreckage had been found. I was appalled by the news and couldn't stop thinking of the wives and relatives of those on board. When we heard the following day that twenty-six of the twenty nine on board had been picked up we were all very relieved. They had been found two hundred miles from the wreckage.

I think everyone on board was affected by this occurrence and although some of them made comments like "these things happen", the news brought home to them the dangers of the job.

The Agent, Diego, came on board that evening I heard that there was to be a Carnival Procession as part of the celebrations in Guaymas, so I asked him when it was. He told me that the big events were taking place on February 1st as in the rest of Mexico. Although we may, therefore, miss it in Guaymas, we may arrive in Ensenada in time to join the fun. I asked him what the carnival was celebrating and I was very interested to learn that the word carnival originated from two Spanish words: carne, meaning meat and Val who was the God of the body as opposed to the soul. The celebrations were, therefore, the feast of the body, the real carnival when people let their hair down prior to forty days of sobriety during Lent.

Although the main festivities weren't taking place until February 1st, there were other events leading up to it. That evening Diego informed me, the big event was cock fighting. When I told him that cock fighting was illegal in Britain he just smiled and said that it was in Mexico too but when Mexicans really want to do something they find means of doing it. Apparently, the cruel sport was so popular that a million pesos (£25,000) was sometimes bet on a single cock.

On the day of our departure from Guaymas, the Saturday, a P and O ship came into the harbour and berthed across the bay from the pipeline wharf. The Engineers had the afternoon off so several of them took the lifeboat and went across to see her officers. They took two boxes of videos with them hoping to swap them. When they returned they told us that it had been virtually deserted but they had managed to swap the videos and so we had some new viewing for our Pacific crossing

We left Guaymas that evening and everyone who wasn't working congregated on the Promenade Deck. I thought that we would get a good view of the town and be able to see the fair in progress but unfortunately, the view was blocked by the grain storage hoppers at first and then by an island, so we returned to our cabins at the end of another day.

CHAPTER 21

ENSENADA AND THE AFTER EFFECT OF RAIN

The one thousand and sixty eight mile trip from Guaymas to Ensenada, around the peninsula of Lower California, was uneventful except for a short stop in the middle of the second night when a fuel pipe burst. We arrived in Ensenada two and a half days later where we went to anchor and waited eagerly for the Agent to come aboard, in the hope that he would bring a stack of mail. Colin and I had only received two letters since Japan and we knew that somewhere in Mexico a large amount of mail was waiting for us. When the news filtered through that in fact there was no mail it was very disappointing. Even the news that there were some newspapers was marred when we realised that they were dated 11th December and therefore nearly two months old!

Ensenada was to be our last port of call in Mexico so we knew that, with luck, the outstanding mail would wait in Mexico until the ship returned and by that time we would have paid off and possibly wouldn't receive the mail at all.

I longed to hear news of home but at least I was with Colin, it must have been far harder for those separated from their loved ones. To lift my spirits I wandered onto deck. Ensenada had recently had heavy rain storms and, whereas on our previous visit, the landscape had been predominantly brown it was now green and vibrant. The rain had brought everything to life, even the highest hillsides were covered with grass. I went ashore soon after we berthed as I wasn't sure how long we would be alongside and because I wanted to walk off the disappointment of receiving no mail. There were large puddles of water stretching out into the road that ran from the docks to the town and all the dirt tracks and yards were quagmires of sticky brown mud. Houses looked as if they'd been washed out and large deposits had been brought down by the rains.

As I wandered around the shops I noticed that there were many special offers on goods to celebrate the Carnival. There were a number of posters in the windows advertising Carnival events but I was surprised to see that, contrary to the information Diego had given me, the first event wasn't taking place until February3rd and that the main Carnival procession and dances were not until the following Sunday February 5th. I didn't stay very long as a huge black cloud lingered over the mountains and threatened another deluge.

It didn't in fact rain at all that day and by the next morning it was so warm that I was comfortable in just a short sleeved blouse. It was perfect weather for walking and so, after spending the last of our pesos which I knew were useless outside Mexico, I set off towards the river and the coast road.

The river was no longer dry and although now it was only about twelve feet wide there were signs that it had recently been a raging torrent stretching from bank to bank and carrying with it everything that got in its way. As the waters had subsided they dropped their load of debris and the whole river bed was littered with branches, rocks, piles of sand, and mud and the occasional dead dog and tin can. The river that now remained was in places two feet deep and surged and foamed as it rushed down towards the sea. It didn't however, daunt the local motorists who still used the roads that ran across the river bed. They forged the water apart and then drove off with dripping mud guards and steaming exhaust pipes. Even the pedestrians picked their way through the mud and debris using numerous rocks as stepping stones, instead of making a detour to the nearest bridge.

I crossed the river on a raised tarmac road that had a pipe running beneath it and so acted as a bridge when the waters were relatively shallow. There were several houses on the far bank but these soon died out and then after a short way I found that I was at the other habitation with just a few meagre houses and a big highway that stretched in front of me. I walked on a little way then crossed the highway to return to the town along the beach. Although I walked on the pavement alongside the beach I disturbed hundreds of sand lizards which had been lazing in the sun on the sand nearby. As I approached they scuttled away and disappeared down scores of holes burrowed in the sand. They moved so fast it was difficult to follow them but I was able to make out that they were about four inches long with vivid yellow eyes. As I approached the town signs were posted on the central reservation identifying it as the Boulevard Lazaro Cardenas and on the left I noticed a naval base built on the sands. A bugler summoned the sailors for inspection but the inspection coincided with the arrival of an ice-cream van and sailors appeared from everywhere to buy ice-cream! There was a goat tethered on a piece of waste land near to the base. He was very flea bitten and dirty but I wondered whether he was a mascot and got tidied up on special occasions to lead the band!

A little further up there was a large paved terrace which fronted three enormous statues. They were sculpted from red stone and were the busts of local dignitaries. All around the terrace there were beds of succulent plants which the recent rains had brought into flower and now they were a mass of colour, each flower daisy-shaped with shiny petals. These were the first flowers except those on trees and shrubs that I had seen in Mexico and it was a lovely sight.

I had nearly reached the road leading to the dock when I noticed a lot of activity on the beach and being my normal curious self I went to investigate. The activity was centred around a gathering of wooden stalls which had been set up on the sands. Some stall holders were selling hamburgers; tortillas; and tacos and clams but most of them seemed to be agents to the local fishing fleet and catches were brought from nearby boats and laid out on the stalls. The whole area was invaded by pelicans and seagulls. They were on the stall roofs on the ground and flapping and reeling in the sky above. It was obvious that here they could get an easy meal as the fish weren't gutted until sold. The birds squawked and screamed like a classful of excited children. They were completely oblivious to personal safety and they just moved a few inches to one side if anyone got too close. Now that I was so close to the pelicans I appreciated their large size, their bodies that were larger than swans and their webbed feet bigger than my hands. I stood watching the spectacle for a long time and the locals and stallholders stood and watched me, so after a while I returned to the ship in the sunshine.

That evening Colin and I went ashore for the last time in Mexico We went with the lads to Hussongs Cantina. We chatted and enjoyed the atmosphere and listened to the wandering singers.

The next day I made sure everything in the cabin was secure in case of bad weather and then at 9.30 p.m. we began our second east/west Pacific crossing.

CHAPTER 22

THE THIRD PACIFIC CROSSING AND THE MARINE TOWER

There are two types of route that can be taken by ships between two points. The first is the great circle which, in effect, is the shortest route because if viewed on the globe it is a straight line. The other is the Rhumb Line which looks like a straight line on a Mercator Chart but is far from it on the globe. Of course, all Great Circles are northward in the Northern Hemisphere and southwards in the Southern Hemisphere. We were advised by the Company's weather routers that the weather in the North was very rough with winds up to Hurricane force and that we should, therefore, follow a series of Rhumb Lines taking us from Ensenada and as far south as Latitude 29 degrees north. This didn't mean, however that we would get good weather but simply the best a wintry North Pacific had to offer. The weather we actually experienced was far from good. For days the Amparo fought against very strong winds and a huge bow swell that reached twenty feet on occasions. The revolutions of the engines had to be reduced because our speed dropped back to twelve knots, and the ship was taking a real pounding.

The movement of the ship, however, was not uncomfortable as she was pitching rather than rolling. It felt like being on a giant see saw. Sometimes, however, when we hit a big wave the 'person' on the other end went a bit crazy and rather than gently bouncing up and down 'he' rocked madly for minutes on an end! Three days later the routers contacted us again and advised to go still further south as far as 27 degrees north. This had the desired effect and on the seventh day we found calmer waters.

When I first heard that the new course would take us between a chain of Sandwich or Hawaiian Islands I thought I would be able to see something of them. I didn't realise that they were so strung out. Even though we were going right through the middle of them the nearest was over sixty miles away.

Midway and Lisyanslin Islands were in fact the closest and I knew that albatross used both islands as breeding grounds. Consequently , as we got closer, more and more birds arrived and started to follow us. At times there were so many weaving and diving in our wake I was surprised they didn't collide with one another.

After several days at sea, a telegram arrived with the news that the Indian crew would be paying off at arrival in Yokohama. They had already been on the ship for ten months and I felt very happy for them, knowing what it was like being parted from families for so long. As we got closer so their excitement increased and often singing and whistling filtered up from the decks below. Life went on as normal for us with everyone into their own routines. Each day we ate slept and worked and socialised as before but as the days went by conversations became more repetitive and jokes were told for the tenth time! I wasn't bored however, as I still had plenty of sewing to do and Spanish to learn and I spring cleaned the cabin from top to bottom. It was nice to be back at sea and into a routine before the next series of ports and shoreside visits, when there would be no routine but just a determination to see as much as possible.

We crossed the International Date Line during the evening of February 12th so we lost February 13th. Soon after the crossing we had to start going northward but luckily the weather stayed reasonably calm and we had a smooth ride until the last day of the passage. During the early hours of the morning a huge swell built up and the wind speed increased. We took it all on the beam and consequently rolled. It took me quite a time to get used to the rolling and I realised during the morning that I had forgotten some of the golden rules during bad weather. Firstly I forgot to keep at least one hand free to steady myself with and when we took a big roll I nearly ended up in the washing machine head first! Secondly I left the electric iron unattended on a smooth surface and it fell off and smashed the handle. The third mistake was to forget to secure everything correctly so the books cascaded off the bookshelf and nearly knocked me out! After that I got used to the rolling.

During the same morning a telegram arrived informing the Captain that the crew would not be paying off on arrival instead the payoff date would be 25th February, a week later. The whistling and singing stopped abruptly.

We arrived at Tokyo Bay pilot at 11.30 p.m. that night but we weren't taken alongside, instead we anchored overnight. Now that we were so close to land we realised how cold it was. Overnight the temperature dropped well below freezing point and as we only had a tiny heater in the bathroom to give us heat, I had to pile blankets on the bunk before I could get to sleep.

The next morning I put on so many clothes that I must have looked like a teddy bear but at least I was warm when I stood on the Promenade Deck to see us go alongside. Tokyo Bay and Yokohama harbour were as full of ships as ever and we had to weave in and out of them to get alongside. When the ship had tied up the agent arrived and we were thrilled to see that he carried four big mail bag. I went back inside to await our mail but I still had to keep on my thick jumper and gloves, it was almost as cold inside as out at 5 degrees centigrade.

Colin and I received thirteen letters. It was really good to get so much news from home at last. It took us over an hour to read them all and it was amazing that so much had happened at home in that time.

During the morning the Engineers worked on the heating system and by mid afternoon a wonderful flow of warm air radiated from the overhead vents and at last we began to thaw out.

As it was Sunday, there was no cargo work but Colin didn't really want to go up the road so he offered to do the on board duties. I decided, however that I would go ashore to buy some presents. I ended up at the Silk Hotel and browsed through the shops. I found a beautiful broach which was black and gold and called a damasene designed jewellery piece. The design was hand created in gold which was then covered in a special lacquer which was then burnt off to give the black effect. The burning process apparently has to be repeated several times to achieve the desired effect. The design is then fixed by boiling the whole thing in green tea. Finally the piece of jewellery is polished using a special charcoal. The result was a beautiful gold bamboo cane and leaf on a matt black background. I was surprised that the process originated from Syria as it was so typically Japanese in its precision and care, it had ,however, been used in Japan for over a thousand years and was to the Orientals a sign or symbol of fortune.

From the Silk centre I returned to the Marine Tower. It was already a hive of activity. There were plenty of visitors and the lifts that took them to the top were moving up and down inside the structure of the Tower. The Tower's main function is as a lighthouse and, standing at one hundred metres high, is the highest lighthouse in the world. However, observation platforms have been built beneath the light which give visitors a 'bird's eye' view of the city of Yokohama. It cost five hundred yen (just over a pound) to get in but that covered a visit to a maritime museum, which is contained in the tower, as well as some concessionary souvenir shops. The lift had windows inside so that the occupants could see the view on the way up but there was hardly time to look around as it only took a few minutes to get to the top.

It was a clear day and from the observation platform I could see the whole city which, according to the guide map, covers 156.6 square miles! There were signs posted round the walls showing the direction of even more distant landmarks including Chiba and Mt. Fuji, but it wasn't clear enough to see that far. As I walked around the tower, however, I could easily pick out China Town and the Isezachi Cho and the foreign cemetery but most of the Amparo was hidden behind a massive warehouse. There was also a good view of Tokyo harbour littered with hundreds of ships at anchor. I took some photos, did several more circuits of the platform and then returned to ground level and the Maritime museum.

The museum housed an excellent array of exhibits. Besides the usual models of ships, boats and barges there were models describing fishing techniques, salt refineries and pearl and seaweed farms. In the fishing section there were models of fish 'houses' (open-sided concrete squares) which were placed on the seabed to encourage fish to the area. There were huge diagrams of whales, one showing all the products made from various parts of the mammal. The pearl farm displays were also very interesting. Diagrams and models explained the whole process: firstly they showed how wild oysters were caught by world famous women divers called 'Ama' who wear cotton robes and goggles for diving. The captured oysters were then used for breeding. The resulting baby oysters were 'cultivated' in a special spot on the ocean bed, and, after three years, beads were planted into the oysters. The beads it explained were in fact the nuclei of a pie-toe shell found in the Mississippi River in America. The method of getting them into the oysters was devised by one Mikimoto and entailed a delicate operation performed by highly trained technicians.

After the operation the oysters were put into wire cages and suspended in the sea from wooden rafts, until they were ready for 'harvesting', three to four years later. Each oyster then contained a beautiful cultured pearl. There were several different kinds of pearl on display in show cases: they were pink, white, blue-baroque and black as well as golden ones, each easily distinguished by the colour of the sheen on their surface.

The next display to catch my eye was the laver farms display. I had heard of laver before and knew it was edible seaweed, but I didn't know that it was cultivated in Japan. The Japanese actually use the sea as a medium for growing food. The models showed how nets made from hemp and coconut palm were hung on frameworks in rows, at a suitable height. In the autumn, spores around stick to the nets and, during the winter, grow. The laver is ready for picking in spring and then after drying in the sun, they are ready to eat in the summer. I spent a long time looking around and when I at last left it was time to return to the ship for lunch. I stayed on the ship for the afternoon and we sailed just after 7 p.m. on course for Yokkachi.

CHAPTER 23

YOKKACHI AND THE PLASTIC LAWN

The weather for the trip up the coast was miserable. Freezing gale-force winds blew all day, but we arrived off Yokkachi according to schedule and anchored overnight in the approaches.

When we were called next morning at 6.00 a.m. I was very reluctant to get up as it was extremely cold in the accommodation and lovely and warm under the blankets in the bunk, so when I looked out of the port to find it was only just getting light, I was very lazy and decided to stay where I was. When I finally did get up we were alongside.

I decided to go ashore at 9.00 a.m. as I knew that we were a long way from the town centre and that the walk would warm me up. I dressed up as if on an expedition to the Arctic and left the ship. It wasn't until I got half way along the quay that I remembered that I didn't have a shore pass. When I got back to the ship I learnt that they hadn't yet arrived on board and so I had to postpone my walk. They didn't actually arrive until after Smoko, so I decided to wait until the afternoon before venturing ashore again.

Straight after lunch I set off again. I passed the hardworking stevedores on the quayside and I walked in the general direction of the town. I had a vague idea where the shops were as I had passed them in the taxi on the way to Nagoya on our previous visit, but I had no map so I didn't know how far it was.

After walking for about half an hour and crossing numerous bridges over water ways, I found the main road which we had driven along to get to Nagoya. It was just as crowded as before with traffic nose-to-tail in both directions. From the main road I knew my way and soon I was passing little streets of wooden houses and their accompanying corner shops. The whole area was obviously very old and very quaint. The shops had modernised a bit but still had wooden facades and several opened on to the street displaying slabs of fish; baskets of fruit and racks of shoes. The shop keepers were dressed up to the eyes in woollen clothes to combat the freezing winds that whistled up their streets.

After walking past several blocks of local shops I arrived at Yokkachi town centre where there were several larger shops and an indoor arcade full of department stores; supermarkets; and Pachinko houses. The whole area was a paradise for window shoppers like me and I browsed for a long time. One of my favourite shops was a confectioners which had a luscious array of homemade sweets and cream cakes.

Bicycles seemed to be the main mode of transport judging from the number of them parked outside the supermarkets and Pachinko houses. Their owners were obviously allowed to use them on the pavements which proved very dangerous for pedestrians. Near the shopping arcade I found a shrine. It was a wooden building with a decorated grey stone roof surrounded by a gravel area, some stone structures that looked a lot like bird baths, which I later discovered were gravestones and a hand washing fountain like the one I'd seen at Kyoto.

On leaving the shrine I decided it was time to make my way back to the ship, and, although, I was tempted to take a taxi I refrained myself and started the long trek back. I was glad I had decided to walk because on the way back I saw two unusual sights. The first was a musical pedestrian crossing. When the lights showed green for pedestrians, a recorder in the traffic lights post played a little tune until it was no longer safe to cross. The second unusual sight was in the garden of one of the old wooden houses. It was a bright lawn made of plastic grass!

Before I reached the docks it started to snow. Although it pitched on my coat it didn't pitch on the ground and by the time I got back to the ship the sun was shining. I had been very impressed with the town of Yokkachi, not only were the shops a perfect integration of old and new but its streets had been spotless despite the surroundings being a mass of heavy industry. It was a model for me of an industrialised town completely functional but clean, tidy and obviously cared for and as such, a compliment to its planners and residents.

That evening some of us were having a quiet pre-dinner drink when we heard news of our pay-off. The Captain told us that he had received a telex which stated that the Company intended to change the officers of the M.V. Amparo at Yokohama around 8th March. We had earlier heard rumours that we might have to re-cross the Pacific and pay-off in Mexico so we were surprised to hear the news. Mostly everyone, however, was pleased and only a few of the single lads who had planned a final fling in Mexico were disappointed. I was pleased although I had thoroughly enjoyed my time on board I longed to see family, friends and house back in England.

CHAPTER 24

KOBE AND THE ACCIDENT

We sailed from Yokkachi that afternoon, February 23rd and arrived at Kobe early the following morning. We were taken alongside the Shiba Pier again and so we were close to the town. During the first morning the crew paid off amidst a mass of confusion, papers and luggage. They eventually left the ship at 11.a.m. and made their way by coach to a local hotel where they had to stay for two days before getting a flight to Bombay.

When they were gone there was no one to serve lunch so I asked the Chief Steward if I could help out but he decided it would be better if everyone helped themselves. As I had already decided to go ashore as soon as possible I left them to it.

As we didn't have long before our pay off I decided it was time to shop for last minute presents. It only took about ten minutes to get to the Sannomiya Shopping street and then I started my search for original presents. The search took me right down Sannomiya Street and the full length of the Motomachi and all the way back under the arches. During the afternoon I also visited the famous Daimaru department stores, it was vast inside with each floor being the size of a normal store, and there were seven of these floors! There was so much to see that I spent a whole hour inside without realising it.

By 3.00 p.m. I was tired of shopping so I went sightseeing instead and headed off in the direction of Ikuta Shrine. It wasn't far from the Sannomiya station and Flower Road but even though it was so close to the hustle and bustle of the city it seemed very remote and within the grounds and around the building itself, it was so quiet you could hear the birds singing in the trees. The Shrine was like a small version of the Heian Shrine at Kyoto. It had curved roofs and its pillars and eaves were painted vermillion red. Its main walls, however, were of plain wood and painted white. It even had a similar decorative gatehouse. As I stood looking at the Shrine two young girls approached. Walked up the steps in front of the building and pulled a long tasselled rope that was hanging at the doorway. The rope was attached to a bell-shaped object which obviously contained a number of balls or beads because when it was shaken it made a noise like a baby's rattle. The girls then stood very still in front of the Shrine as if they were praying. After several minutes they turned, walked down the steps and returned to the hustle and bustle of the city.

When I got back to the ship, the new crew had arrived. The stewards were making a gallant effort to get accustomed to their new surroundings. They must have been very weary after their twenty-four hour journey from Bombay and they were obviously finding it chilly after their own hot climate. They did very well, however, and dinner was served on time and without problems.

The next day a terrible accident happened. The Second Mate, who was helping the new crew rig a derrick, got his hand caught between a block and a wire. Amidst all the confusion no one really how it had happened and it was obvious that he had lost at least two fingers. He was in a terrible state of shock and worried about being able to continue with his career. His fingers were still inside his severed glove so it was retrieved from the deck, almost immediately a taxi arrived to take him to the hospital and Colin went with him.

We didn't know for several hours what was happening and, of course, everyone was very upset and concerned about the incident. It brought home to us all the dangers of shipboard life and showed how easily accidents could happen. The accident happened at 12.30 p.m. but Colin didn't get back to the ship until gone 6 p.m. Then, at last, we had news of his condition. Apparently two of the fingers had been squeezed off and it had been impossible to put them back on, bur the doctors had been able to save the third finger even though it had been badly injured. It was too early to know whether he would be able to continue with his career but we all hoped and prayed that he would make a good recovery, after a period of convalescence and possible physiotherapy, he would be able to return to sea. Colin had stayed with him until he was safely transferred to an International hospital where many could speak English.

The next morning I went with Colin to take him a few essentials and to see how he was. We were both very relieved to see that he had recovered remarkably well from the shock and he wasn't in any pain as he was being given pain killers. The hospital was very pleasantly situated half way up the side of Mt Rokko. There were many nurses dressed in pure white uniforms and they all seemed to be able to speak English. There was even the typical clean 'hospital' smell and everyone was kind and helpful.

When we left the hospital I knew that he was in good hands and that everything possible would be done for him. After such a horrible experience he deserved both.

The Mate was doing the 'on board' duties for the morning as , of course, there were now only two Mates left on board. Colin wanted to trade in his camera for a better one so we decided to go straight from the hospital to the second hand shops 'under the arches'. Colin was lucky and he got a very good deal and ended up with a much better camera. We walked back up the Motomachi and then got a taxi back to the ship in time for Colin to take over the afternoon duties.

When we got back, the ship was 'blacked out' as the Engineers were working on a part of the engine. It was just like being aboard a 'ghost' ship. Everything echoed and it was so quiet that it seemed eerie. The only light was from emergency bulbs in the alleyways, and there was no heating. The cooking equipment was also out of action, of course, so a lunch of cold meats and salad had been prepared. I spent the afternoon in the cabin wrapped up in blankets, jumpers and gloves to keep warm!

The power was eventually switched back on at 6.00 p.m. and by 7.00p.m. I had thawed out and we were sitting down to a hot meal of steak and chips.

That evening Colin and I went to the Seaman's Mission which, in Kobe, was run by both the Church of England's Flying Angel Organisation and the Roman Catholic's Stella Maris. I knew that there were Seaman's Missions in many of the major ports of the world and that they did marvellous work providing advice and facilities for seamen. Several of our colleagues had been to the Kobe Mission before and knew the padre, Ken. He and his wife had been at Kobe for four years as well as well as running missions in several other countries. They were tremendous people and we were very glad to have met them. As soon as Ken heard of the Second Mate's injury he had gone to the hospital to see him and ask if he needed anything and we knew that he would visit him every day until he left Kobe.

The Mission building contained a lounge with a bar, and a games room which was very homely. We sat and talked to Ken and his wife while in the background a young couple with a guitar gave live entertainment. Seamen wandered in and out knowing that they would always be welcome.

We talked until after 11.30 p.m., although the Mission normally closed at 10.30 p.m. but eventually we decided it was time to go and we got a taxi back to the ship.

The Second Mate's accident seemed to have cast a shadow over the whole ship but life had to go on and there was even more work to do. The Mate and Colin now had to work cargo watches between them and as the stevedores worked twenty four hours a day it was decided that the Mate would do the days and Colin the nights. Of course, there was a considerable amount of paperwork too and I offered to help in any way that I could. At first, however, there wasn't anything that I could do so I decided to visit Nunobuki Falls while I had the opportunity. Armed with Colin's new camera and a pair of reliable walking shoes, I set off.

The map showed that the falls were on the slopes of the mountain behind the Shin Kobe Railway Station which was a long way to walk . The exercise would be good for me so I started to walk. After passing Sannomiya I got a bit lost in a maze of small streets but I managed to keep my sense of direction and emerged onto the main road that ran parallel to the station. After walking along the road that ran beneath the railway I came across a map of the falls and followed one of the well marked paths towards the river. The path soon became stepped and was very steep so I had to keep stopping to catch my breath. However, after about ten minutes, I came to the first falls. It was a single cascade of water which fell about ten feet into a pool. There was a covered bridge over the pools I was able to get a good view of the waterfall. The path led upwards again, so I climbed and this time discovered a double fall of water each stage dropping about twelve feet. The higher I got the more water there was and it crashed and bubbled as it dropped over the falls. The path was now fenced to prevent anyone falling in the water. The fence was made of the same artificial wood that I had seen in the Sankei-en gardens in Yokohama and which I had thought was real wood because it looked so authentic.

After climbing upwards again, the path eventually levelled off and I came to the highest falls. They were very spectacular. The water cascaded from the rocks above and fell at least forty feet into a foaming pool below. There were two small stone Buddha's on a rock near the falls, which were surrounded with vases of flowers and burning joss sticks. The whole scene was very beautiful and I made good use of Colin's new camera. The path still led upwards but soon it wound around the mountain and I lost sight of the falls. I climbed on a little further until I came to a group of shelters which overlooked the town of Kobe. There was quite a good view but it was a bit hazy so you couldn't see it clearly. After taking a breather, I decided to go back to the town and took a different path down the mountain. On the way I passed an elderly Japanese man who was playing on a long flute-type instrument. The instrument had a very deep reedy sound which seemed to float in the air. I could still hear its strange sound several feet below.

When I got back to the station, I decided to have a rest from walking so I got a taxi to the Sannomiya Shopping Street. I was a determined to get my last-minute presents and, after walking the entire length of Sannomiya and Motomachi Streets, I ended up with some Japanese biscuits, a skier/balancer, and a pen with a light in it. At last I had presents for everyone.

When I got back to the ship there was some typing for me to do and I was pleased that I was able to help. During the day several of the ship's crew went to visit the Second Mate. They returned with the news that he was fairly bright, although he was being given plenty of painkillers, which he needed.

Our whole stay in Kobe seemed to have been jinxed. Something seemed to happen every day and the next day was no exception. The Mate discovered that someone, probably one of the crew who had paid off, had put rice down the drains. This meant that scores of plumbing pipes would have to be dismantled which was yet another burden for the overworked deck crew, the Mate and Colin.

We heard that it was planned for cargo to be finished by 3.00 a.m. and that the ship would sail immediately for Katgowa, so that we could beat another ship to the berth and save four days at anchor. Cargo kept coming aboard all day. There were cars; caterpillar tractors; steel structures; and parts of a huge electrical plant bound for Manzanillo, which had originally represented 70,000 tons of cargo but which mostly had been taken by other ships previously. Everything went reasonably well until teatime and then the weather changed, it poured with rain and there was thunder and lightning. The crew started to close the hatches immediately but as soon as they were closed, it stopped raining and they all had to be opened again.

The Mate had been working since 6.00 a.m. and had been hassled by officials all day, by dinnertime he was about at the end of his tether. Colin had been working during the morning doing paperwork and then he took over from the Mate to do the night.

Some of the lads had promised to play darts at the Mission and asked if I would like to go with them and it was really a relief to get off the ship.

We went first to the Sapporo beer hall which was a large room containing scores of wooden tables and chairs decorated in the style of a German Beer Keller. The beer was served in huge glasses called steins, which must have held more than two litres. Luckily they sold it in smaller glasses! I don't think I could have tackled a stein. After a while three more Engineers arrived. They had been to the hospital to see the Second Mate and they said he was trying to keep cheerful but knew that he would miss the visitors when the ship left.

We felt very sorry for him but we knew that Ken would visit every day and for that we were very grateful.

When we had finished our drinks, we went to the Mission to play in the darts match. We lost every game but we had a very sociable time and enjoyed chatting with the several English people who were there. Some of them were from other ships but others were residents in Japan and found the

Mission a good place to meet fellow English men and women.

I left with the Junior Chief Engineer around 10 p.m. and returned to the ship. Colin was in the midst of a huge stack of papers trying to work out somewhere to put four caterpillar tractors, which wouldn't fit in Hold Number 4. In the end they had to be lashed on deck.

They continued loading all night and managed to finish in time for the 3.00 a.m. sailing, but the jinx proved itself again and when the engines were tested, prior to leaving, it was found that a cylinder head had cracked so we had to stay where we were.

The engineers worked through the night and until 2.30 p.m. the following day. Colin managed to get to bed about 4.00 a.m. and at least the breakdown meant that he and the Mate would have a short while in which to recuperate before the next onslaught.

It seemed that while we were still at Kobe the bad luck continued because during the morning I heard that the Junior Chief Engineer had been taken to the Doctor's feeling unwell. We knew that he had suffered a heart attack a few years previously and we were all very concerned. The Doctor diagnosed high blood pressure but said that his heart was all right and fortunately he was allowed back on the ship with instructions to take life a bit easier! I wouldn't have been surprised if we were all suffering from high blood pressure after the events of the previous few days!

We eventually left Kobe just after 3.00 p.m. and I, for one, heaved a great sigh of relief!

CHAPTER 25

KAKAGOWA, KUDAMATSU AND THE FRIENDLY PEOPLE

It only took us two hours to reach Kakagowa as it was only a thirty mile hop up the coast through part of the Inland Sea, however, because of our delay we had to go to anchor. In the meantime we received another telex from the company saying that they were planning our pay off for 9th March and that the new Second Mate would be arriving early the following day. I think that after the events of the previous few days everyone was looking forward to the pay off and although we were running behind schedule, we hoped the change would not be delayed.

While we were at anchor the Captain did Colin's watch and Colin did the Second Mate's twelve to four watches. It seemed strange to turn in at 7.30 p.m. and get up at quarter to midnight but we soon got adjusted. I did my washing and cleaned the bar then spent the remainder of the time on the bridge with Colin. The ship was deadly quiet at that time in the morning as everyone else was asleep!

At 4.30 a.m. we went back to bed and slept until 9.30 a.m.. Colin spent the rest of the morning preparing for the handover to the next officer and I started to sort out our gear ready for packing.

We stayed at anchor until 7.30 a.m. the next morning. Colin and I had gone to bed at 4.30 a.m. after the twelve to four watch but of course, Colin was needed for standby again at 7.15 a.m.

Kakagowa port was similar to Nagoya. The docks themselves were miles from the actual town and the whole area was a mass of industry. It was smaller than Nagoya, however, with only two quays. The loading started almost immediately The cargo was sheets of steel which had arrived from nearby factories on railway carriages pulled by an ingenious radio-controlled train. The driver could sit wherever he liked on the train or even get off it and stand nearby because he carried the controls with him in a little yellow box. Shoreside swan-necked cranes were used to loan neatly packaged loads of steel.

When everything was arranged Colin and I went back to bed but it was impossible to sleep because of the noise going on outside. That afternoon the new Second Mate arrived. The Mate and Colin were especially pleased to see him as they could at last go back to doing their own jobs.

Colin worked the evening shift from 4.00 p.m. to midnight. I had planned an early night to catch up on sleep but was persuaded instead to help some engineers drink two bottles of excellent German wine. We had a very sociable evening and I certainly slept well when I eventually did get to bed around 11.00 p.m. The stevedores finished the cargo at 3.00 a.m. the following morning and we sailed three hours later. When Colin was called at 6.30 a.m. I had every intention of getting up too but as it was still dark and pouring with rain I just turned over and went back to sleep!

The passage to our next stop, Kudamatsu, was through Naikai, the Inland Sea, so we carried a pilot for the whole passage. During the day we passed scores of islands and even more ships and coasters. It continued to rain and visibility was reduced quite considerably. That night we anchored off Kudamatsu as there was no empty berth for us, however, one of the ships that was alongside sailed at 11.00 a.m. the next morning so we took her place.

The weather had changed dramatically. The sun now shone brilliantly in a clear blue sky and we all congregated on the promenade deck to watch us go alongside. As we got closer, we could see scores of people fishing from the end of the quay. As soon as I'd had my lunch, I decided to take advantage of the lovely weather to go ashore. The wind was quite chilly but the sun was so warm I hardly noticed it. When I was halfway down the quay a man drew up in his car and offered me a lift to town. I hesitated, at first, but he could speak perfect English and was obviously just being kind, so I accepted. He drove me to Kudamatsu station in the centre of the town. I thanked him for his kindness as he drove off.

I found that Kudamatsu was a charming little town. Behind its façade of factories and worker's apartments it was old and quaint. The streets were very narrow, hardly wide enough for one car, and lined with old style wooden houses which had decorative lead roofs carved at the edges and traditional paper-thin wooden walls. Most of the houses had enchanting little gardens filled with fir trees, orange bushes and dog kennels, some even contained small shrines and vermillioned bridges. The shops were dotted around amongst the houses. There were several confectioners which offered an assortment of delicious cakes and sweets and also one that sold beautifully made paper flowers.

The shopping streets were virtually deserted except for a few mothers who were sitting with their children playing in the sun. Everyone was extremely friendly and smiled as I walked by. I returned the smiles and when some small children said, 'hello, hello' I said 'hello' too. Halfway down one of the streets I found a chemist and went inside to buy some toothpaste. I was served by a charming elderly lady just as friendly as everyone else. She was wearing a dark kimono covered by a brilliantly white frilly pinafore. I pointed to the boxes of toothpaste and she made a gesture of 'help yourself'. When I had selected the one I wanted she showed me the price tag and I paid her the money. She smiled all the time, even her eyes smiled. When I left she bowed again and again and we exchanged numerous 'arigatos' and smiles. After a while I made my way back to the ship past the streets of quaint old houses. As I walked along in the warm sunshine surrounded by friendly people I felt very happy.

When I got back to the ship, the stevedores were loading paraffin wax like it had gone out of fashion and by 5.30 p.m. we were ready to leave.

Our route to Nagasaki took us through the remainder of the Inland Sea and through the Kammon Straits, a narrow stretch of water between the islands of Honshu and Kyushu. I watched our passage through the straits from the cabin. Before opening the shutters I was careful to turn off all the lights to prevent distracting the pilot and the officers on the bridge. As we approached so more lights appeared and soon there were lights everywhere. There were shoreside lights, street lamps; house lights, passing cars lights, neon advertising lights, aircraft warning lights on high buildings and radio masts. There were also scores of lights on buoys and in lighthouses, and navigation lights on the mass of coasters, boats and ships surrounding us.

A bridge spanned the straits at their narrowest point between the towns of Shimonoseki and Moji. The bridge was also well lit with bulbs at regular intervals so that it looked like a long Christmas tree. Great care had to be taken as we passed under the bridge, not only to make sure we kept clear of the rocks on either side but to avoid the many vessels that were coming in the other direction. It took us over an hour to get clear of the straits and then another nine hours to reach Nagasaki approaches.

CHAPTER 26

NAGASAKI AND THE PHOTOGRAPH

The Nagasaki pilot arrived just after 7.00 a.m. and Colin was called to go to the bridge. I dressed hurriedly and then went out on the promenade deck to watch us go alongside. The harbour was surrounded with picturesque craggy islands, which had, rough covering of trees and scrubby grass. We passed an enormous shipbuilding yard. The dry dock there could, apparently accommodate ships up to a million tons deadweight, although as far as I knew there were no ships of that size in existence!

On one of the nearby islands I could see a tiny village. Above the village on the side of a hill, was a small white Catholic church. I knew from reading the book Shogun, that Nagasaki had been the gateway for Western influence in Japan and the birthplace of Christianity in the country but it still seemed strange to see such a church on Japanese soil.

The pilot used the same tactics to get alongside as the one in Kudamatsu had used on our visit there. He simply steered the ship straight for the quay and at the last minute went full astern and turned the rudder. Unfortunately on this occasion he misjudged his distances and we hit the quay with a resounding bang! A strong shockwave passed through the ship but luckily the Amparo had a reinforced bow and only suffered a small dent, even the quay remained intact.

As soon as we were tied up the stevedores boarded. Our cargo, the remainder of the electric plant for Manzanillo, was lined up on the quay amongst thousands of pieces of other electrical plants. When everything was ready, mobile cranes were used to place the required pieces to the ship's side and they were taken aboard and stowed. I had noticed in other ports, because the winchman couldn't see what was happening below from their position at the winches, each gang employed a man who instructed them using pre-arranged hand signals. At Nagasaki it was the same but as well as using hand signals they used whistles, a different number of blasts indicating different requirements. During our three and a half day stay we got used to the shrill series of whistles that always accompanied the whirring winches when cargo was being worked.

I had planned to go ashore that first afternoon as there were several things I wanted to see in Nagasaki. A kindly Japanese man had brought a whole stack of maps and information pamphlets for us to use, so I knew exactly where to go. Unfortunately, however the Immigration officials weren't so efficient and our passes didn't arrive until very late in the afternoon and I had to postpone my visiting until the following day. It came round eventually and I made my way towards the Peace Park, my first stop. An elderly woman helped me on my journey there noticing I was a bit lost.

The Peace Park was just across the road from the streetcar stop and as I crossed the road and made my way to the flight of stairs that led to the hillside park I knew I was walking over the area that had been most affected by the blast of the nuclear bomb, and it made me shudder. At the top of the stairs was the Peace Fountain. A notice nearby explained its origins: 'It read: August 9th 1945. Many people burnt all over by the bomb blast died crying for water. Remembering this, their last desire, and praying for the souls of those victims, we offer them this fountain also with prayer for everlasting peace. The National Council for Peace and against Nuclear Weapons and Nagasaki City constructed the fountain here in the Peace Park with contributions from all over the country. I wish everyone here to pray for the souls of the dead and World Peace.'

Mayor of Nagasaki

The fountain is eighteen meters in diameter, seven meters in height and was completed in August 1969 The water springs up in the form of flying wings as of the dive of peace and the cranes, which symbolise the shape of Nagasaki harbour. There were seats around the fountain and sitting on one with her head buried in her hands was an elderly lady. As I felt the dreadful mourning, I could have cried too and I certainly prayed for World Peace.

Then a very moving experience took place. As I walked around the fountain, four middle aged Japanese approached me and one asked me, in sign language, if I would stand with them to have my photograph taken. They were obviously all old enough to remember the bombing and I was truly amazed at their forgiveness and kindliness. I held out my hand to one of the men, and as the picture was being taken, we stood hand in hand smiling. I was very proud to be able to show my friendship in such a way and it made me realise that world peace is not an impossible dream.

Beyond the fountain was an area of open land. It had tough patchy grass and several trees that had been planted but none seemed to be growing very healthily and some of the leaves on the trees were brown and there were large patches of bare earth where nothing was growing. There were a number of women, old enough to remember the fated day, busily pulling up weeds from the rough grass like they were determined to allow it to grow as well as possible.

At the opposite end of the park was the Peace Statue. A board was posted nearby and it read:' The Peace Statue. The people of Nagasaki built this statue to symbolise and appeal for everlasting peace in August 1955, the 10th Anniversary of the atomic bombing which caused the people of Nagasaki to experience the unbelievable tragedy and lost great numbers of people. This 10 meter high bronze statue was completed by an authoritative sculptor, Mr Seibo Litamura, through both foreign and domestic contributions. The right hand pointing to the sky tells of the atomic bomb threat; the left one stretching horizontally shows tranquil peace. Its solid built body is the dignity of God. The gentle face the symbol of Divine love; the fast closed eyes pray for the repose of war victim's souls; while the folded right leg shows meditation or quiescence and the bent left one shows help or movement. This is an unparalleled work of art in the world, in its scale and conceptions.

In front of the enormous statue was a large black coffin.

I returned to the streetcar after leaving the park and then walked to the site of the Martyrdom of 26 Saints. It was situated on a steep hill opposite Nagasaki Railway Station. At the top of the hill I found a monument to the Martyrs, overlooked by a quaint little Catholic church. The church had two spires which looked like half-used candles covered in dripped candle wax. On one was painted the word SANCTUS and on the other SANCTE.

The Monument itself was built into a wall in the shape of a cross. Along the horizontal of the cross were life-size statues of the Martyrs. A notice nearby explained that the Martyrs were foreign missionaries and along with twenty Japanese converts had been crucified in Nagasaki on February 5th 1597, after being arrested in Kyoto and Osaka. They had apparently been breaking a decree outlawing Christianity in Japan at that time. They were canonised in 1862 by Pope Pius IX in remembrance of their bravery. The Monument to their memory had been constructed in 1962.

From the hillside I was able to see a panoramic view of the town and harbour and the enormous Mitsubishi shipyard. It was hard to imagine that the whole area had been razed to the ground by the bomb blast.

I decided to walk back to the town centre as so often before I'd seen things that I would have missed if I'd taken a taxi or a bus. It was the same in Nagasaki. By walking I found a very old beautiful part of the town which was obviously untouched by the bomb. They were on the far banks of the river. In places the river was spanned beautiful stone bridges, many of which were arched and carved. From one of the bridges I looked down into the water and noticed scores of Koi carp swimming around in it. Several houses backed right onto the river and their waste water simply flowed from pipes into the river so I was amazed that the fish could survive in the fetid trickling water. I crossed the bridge and walked amongst the old houses. Nearly all of them were traditionally built with curving roofs and thin walls. They were gathered around narrow streets and I followed one of the streets which led to a beautiful old temple, Kofuking Temple, which was a gathering of buildings, shrines, steps, gates and grave stones all beautifully built and preserved. A strong smell of burning incense wafted from the shrines.

After walking along several more narrow streets I found the main shopping area and the huge Hamamachi Shopping Street which was similar to the Motomachi at Kobe. During the day I had seen many disabled people and in the Hamamachi I saw more. They were people with thick bandages and dark glasses, people with skin diseases and I knew that all the handicaps were the effects of the atom bomb and radiation. I couldn't help wondering that if everyone in the world was to visit Nagasaki it would help in the abolition of the atomic bomb and determination of world peace.

I bought a few postcards and admired the large displays of famous Nagasaki tortoiseshell goods and then took a taxi back to the ship.

Colin had the rest of the afternoon off and as he wanted to see the Peace Park we called a taxi which took us there. The Peace Park had the same effect on Colin as it did on me. Since my visit the day before I learnt that there was a museum containing the relics of the dreadful bombing and so we decided to go there too. It was housed in the International Culture Hall which was near to the Peace Park. On the way to it we passed the epicentre of the blast. There were large signs posted listing the horrific facts like: 300000 degrees centigrade temperatures; 11574 houses burnt down; 1326 ruined; 5500 half-ruined; 73884 people killed and 74,909 injured.

There was a tall jet-black obelisk built beneath the exact spot of the 16000 foot explosion and nearby a solitary church pillar which had miraculously remained intact. We climbed a flight of steps behind the obelisk and found the International Centre. Inside there were four floors of relics and photographs portraying the extent of the damage and suffering. The exhibits were absolutely horrifying and, at times, as we wandered from one to another I felt physically sick.

On display there were stone roof tiles blistered and scorched by the immense heat, there were shreds of clothing taken from the victims; there were stone and pillars taken from the famous Urahami church,; there were completely unrecognisable lumps of melted glass which had once been bottles; there were wooden walls of houses which had been several kilometres from the epicentre and yet were burnt and scorched except in the places protected by articles and people standing in front of them at the exact time of the blast, 11.02 a.m.. The shadows of articles and people remained on the wood. There was even a clock which although it was smashed and scorched, showed the exact time of the blast There were also scores of photographs taken shortly after the terrible event. There was an aerial view of Nagasaki which was just a flattened heap of rubble.

There were photographs of smouldering ruins; burnt emaciated bodies lying in the streets, and worst of all were the photographs of the wounded who had massive raw patches on their bodies, scorched faces and weeping wounds. Several were crying out for mercy and relief from the pain, others just stared blankly into space, so terribly burnt and scorched that they were beyond caring. There was also quite a large display showing the after effects of radiation poisoning and burning, huge puckered outbreakings on the skin and hair loss.

Finally on the fourth floor were photographs of the opening of the Peace Park and of International conferences and meetings seeking world peace and the abolition of Nuclear weapons.

Afterwards, standing outside in the warm afternoon sunshine it was difficult to imagine the dreadful suffering and destruction but both Colin and I knew that our visit to the museum and surrounding area would have a lasting effect on us both.

CHAPTER 27

YOKOHAMA AND PAY OFF DAY

There were a few delays caused by the heavy rain showers, but, eventually Nagasaki cargo was all aboard and we set sail at 7.45 p.m. on 9th March bound for Yokohama and home!

The one day, fifteen-hour passage was quite tough but I was so excited about going home and so busy packing and cleaning that I hardly noticed.

We arrived at No.1 Buoy, Tokyo Bay at 4.30 p.m. on 11th March and, after anchoring for two and a half hours, we were taken alongside. While we were at anchor I worked out the details of the trip and pinned them up in the bar. They read: days on board: 145; days at sea: 75; days in port: 59; days at anchor: 7; days under pilotage 4; total distance steamed: 28,184 nautical miles.

That night we had a big pay off party. Several of us had bought crisps; and peanuts and we piled them onto plates and handed them round. There was plenty of beer and other drinks flowing and by 1.00 a.m. on Sunday morning everyone was singing and reminiscing happily.

Sunday 12th March, our last day on the M.V. Amparo, dawned cloudy and wet and several felt the same way when we woke up, but we soon realised it was pay off day and felt much better. I finished packing during the morning and had everything ready to move out by the time the new officers arrived just after smoko.

Each relief was ferried off and shown around and finally a hand over list was signed. Our first flight wasn't until 10.30 p.m. that evening but as the cook couldn't cope with double numbers for evening meal, a coach arrived at 3.00 p.m. to take us to the Silk Centre for a meal.

Our cases were winched ashore and then we grabbed our hand luggage and made for the gangway. I couldn't help feeling a little nostalgic as I left the ship. I'd had a marvellous time aboard and seen many wonderful things and it was unlikely that I would ever see the M.V. Amparo again.

As the coach pulled away we waved enthusiastically at the new officers and Indian crew who lined the rails and then we sped down the quay. As the ship disappeared into the distance I knew that I would never forget her and my five months afloat. There had been good and bad things about the trip as with all experiences, but I knew that in time I would only remember the good ones and, after all, they had been very good ones as a wife on the ocean waves!